D0858910

Orangutans
My Cousins, My Friends

A journey to understand and
save the person of the forest

LEIF COCKS

First Published in 2016 by
The Orangutan Project
PO Box 1414
South Perth WA 6951 Australia
www.orangutan.org.au

National Library of Australia Cataloguing-in-Publication data:

ISBN: 978-0-9954080-1-2 (paperback edition)
ISBN: 978-0-9954080-0-5 (e book)

Cover photograph by The Orangutan Project

All profits from the sale of this book will go towards orangutan conservation projects to ensure their survival in the wild.

Printed by EnviroPrint Australia on 100% recycled post consumer waste paper made carbon neutral.

DEDICATION

I dedicate this book to all orangutans.
May it be that one day you will all live safe and free.

ACKNOWLEDGEMENTS

I would like to acknowledge all those who have shared, and continue to share, my journey to save orangutans.

In particular, The Orangutans Project's board, staff, contractors, volunteers and donors. You are both my inspiration and my friends. Thank you.

I would also like to thank, Jennifer Marr, for helping me to share the story of my friends, the orangutans, and in doing so, speak up for those who can't speak for themselves.

CONTENTS

FOREWORD

By Clare Campbell, Executive Director, Wildlife Asia

As humans, each of us share 97% of our genetic make-up with orangutans, therefore we are literally 97% orangutan and 3% human. However this uniquely human 3% does not grant us superiority, but rather responsibility.

For Leif Cocks, this sense of responsibility has translated into a lifelong dedication to this species which he affectionately and quite accurately calls, *our orange cousins.*

Most of us cannot help but feel love and empathy for a being so kindred. They really are like holding up a mirror and seeing a better, kinder version of ourselves.

Perhaps because of our close kinship, their predicament only serves to reinforce this recognition as our generation is witnessing the rapid demise of the orangutan at the hands of human greed and our incessant need for growth. For most, the knowledge that we in fact contribute to this evokes a degree of shame and a desire to, at the very least, compensate for our choices and behaviour.

As conservationists our task is not only to strategize the protection of orangutans in the wild, but to determine how to harness this despair and to foster the altruism within our community to translate it into real and effective contribution, on behalf of our donors and supporters.

Leif's ability to do this has been remarkable. His understanding of human behaviour parallels his knowledge of orangutans. His evolving philosophies and insights into emotional intelligence have enabled such an enormously successful journey through The Orangutan Project. A journey that has created a movement of change makers and generated a level of financial support that is genuinely challenging the threats to orangutans and their habitat.

For me, forging my own path in conservation, under Leif's guidance and mentorship, has been fuelled with inspiration, unwavering perseverance, strength and optimism.

To be honest, conservation is a tough game. It's not so much a career path we choose but perhaps a path we are chosen to walk. Leif has led me, and many others, on that path with integrity, on his selfless mission to build The Orangutan Project into a highly effective vehicle with which to drive forward the conservation of orangutans.

Now the foremost orangutan conservation organisation in the world, The Orangutan Project and its achievements are to be applauded. For Leif and his team though, success will only really be celebrated when the orangutans no longer need their help.

Until then, I continue to walk by his side and together we will all ensure that the orangutans still stand a fighting chance.

INTRODUCTION...

*"We must be willing to let go of the life we planned so as
to have the life that is waiting for us."*
Joseph Campbell

I am often asked why I choose to work for orangutans.

And my honest answer is, that in many ways, it was the orangutans who first chose me.

As I'm sure you can imagine, my answer is often met with quizzical looks, raised eyebrows and an even greater curiosity on the part of the questioner. But the truth is that I never consciously planned to do this work. Nor did I envision myself as becoming an author, a speaker or an outspoken campaigner on their behalf. And I certainly had no idea that I would one day found and lead an international conservation charity, The Orangutan Project, to ensure the welfare and survival of our remarkable orange cousins.

However, from experience, I've come to see that life has a way of putting unexpected possibilities and significant choices across our paths, and the decision is always our individual responsibility as to how we will respond. So it was for me, that by the time we started The Orangutan Project back in 1998, it had become the single, most obvious course of action for me to take. In fact, to *not start* the organisation and dedicate my life to this work was simply no-longer an option. This was because by this stage in my journey as a zoologist, primate keeper and an orangutan specialist, I had become intimately aware of the suffering of orangutans in captivity and had experienced first-hand, their increasingly precarious situation in the wild.

Interestingly, I did not come to this point of view in one blinding flash of insight nor in a single turning point moment. Instead my choice to start The Orangutan Project happened more as a process of learning over a number of years. In many ways it was almost a natural evolution within me, as I experienced a unique set of personal encounters and professional circumstances where I became more and more uncomfortably aware of what was happening to orangutans around the world.

However, if I had to select the most impacting and formative events which occurred during this time, it would definitely have to be my meetings with two very different orangutans. One born in the wild and the other in captivity. Both whom lived worlds apart and on two separate continents. It was their stories and their fates which ultimately created the defining shift in my perspective.

Perth's Rescue...

I first heard of this young, wild born male orangutan whilst on a working tour of orangutan rehabilitation centres and sanctuaries in Central Kalimantan in 1996. At the time I had been a primate zookeeper at Perth Zoo for over eight years and had come to know and love the captive orangutans in my care. On the other hand, I had also begun volunteering and visiting rescue and rehabilitation centres, as well as spending time with wild orangutans in both Indonesia and Malaysia during my annual leave... as I was committed to help orangutans in whatever way I could.

However, on this occasion I had been asked to lead an educational tour and visit renowned orangutan pioneer Dr Birute Galdikas with a group of volunteers from Perth Zoo. So I jumped at the chance to go back into the field, as the aim of our time away was to support the valuable work in the rescue, rehabilitation and re-release of orangutans into the wild. It was whilst we were in Central Kalimantan that Birute and I were told about a six year old orangutan being held in a small cage in the back of a local bitumen factory. As is usual in these cases, the young orangutan's mother was slaughtered in front of the helpless infant, and in this instance, the orphaned baby was then held in the back of a bitumen factory as a pet.

Now even though, for private individuals, the practice of holding orangutans captive is illegal within Indonesia, it is an all too common occurrence amongst many of the higher ranking locals and military officials within the country. This is because it is seen as a mark of power for anyone able to keep an orangutan as a pet and to so clearly flout the local laws in such a blatant manner. In addition to this, "owning" an orangutan is also seen as a money making opportunity, due to the lucrative black market for baby orangutans in the illegal pet trade. One of the problems with confiscation is, unless the asking price is paid, the owner will often poison and kill the orangutan rather than allow its release to anyone else.

However, the one small piece of good news here is that, registered orangutan welfare organisations can execute rescue confiscations of any illegally held orangutans with the approval of the Ministry of Forestry. So with the facts of the situation foremost in our minds, we immediately arranged a surprise confiscation raid at the bitumen factory to give the owner no time to poison the orangutan. Our plan was to head straight to the factory and locate the caged orangutan within the building. Once this was done, Birute would go and get the police and forestry officials to assist us with the orangutan's removal and I would stand guard over the cage to prevent any harm coming to our precious charge until they arrived.

Fortunately our surprise mission went according to plan and after some negotiation between the authorities and the very disgruntled bitumen factory owner, we were able to get permission to break open the lock on the cage and release the orangutan held captive inside. It's important to note that the release of a once wild but long caged orangutan, can be an unpredictable event, as there is no way of knowing how a newly freed orangutan will respond. But using the practical knowledge and experience I had from working with the orangutans at the zoo, we worked with the learned survival skills of the species. This dictates that they stay off the ground as much as possible and remain safely in the tree canopy above their jungle home. Knowing this, I tried to create an environment outside the cage which would encourage the orangutan to run towards me for safety.

As soon as the lock was cut and the cage door swung open, our intelligent yet nervous young orangutan immediately tried to clamber to freedom. As he left the cage, I managed is scoop him up in my arms and held him there. I then strategically positioned myself by standing in the middle of an open area, near the cage, making my body the safest place for him to be. This was where he stayed, attached and tenaciously clinging onto me for the couple of days that it took for us to travel by car to the nearest rescue and rehabilitation centre.

Finally we were able to hand this young orangutan -who by this time was renamed *Perth*, after my home town and the zoo at which I worked – over to the Pangkalan Bun Rescue Centre team. We were happy that we could help save Perth from his cruel captivity and we knew that the rescue centre would be able to work with him to teach him the skills necessary for him to survive back out in the wild. Ultimately we hoped that Perth would one day be released into a secure forest environment where he could live free and safe from human interference.

Over the next year or so I stayed in contact with the Pangkalan Bun Rescue Centre to hear how Perth was progressing. Finally, I was overjoyed to hear that he had been released back to a protected piece of forest habitat as a free and wild orangutan. To have this news gave me some comfort that at least, on a personal level, I could still do something to improve the situation for the orangutans in Kalimantan. By doing so, even in this small way, I could help the population of wild orangutans maintain their grip on survival.

Unfortunately, this wasn't the end of Perth's story or the last time that I would hear of his contact with humans. This was because, unlike the female of the species, who tend to stay within a fixed and stable territorial area, wild male orangutans are likely to wander across large territories and roam freely through expansive tracts of jungle forest. So it was that, soon after his release, Perth managed to wander outside his protected forest sanctuary. Once outside the boundary of safety he encountered some illegal loggers who mercilessly set upon him with machetes. The result being that Perth was severely injured before he was able to escape his attackers.

However, as the intelligent and aware being he was, Perth knew there was one place where he would be safe, one place where humans would help him instead of hurt him. So remarkably and against all odds, Perth was able to drag his bleeding and battered body back to the release site and this is where the staff found him in a poor condition, but still alive.

I can tell you that the wonderful team at the centre was able to save Perth's life that day and eventually return him once more to a state of physical health. Ultimately they even facilitated a second release for him into a more protected forest sanctuary.

However, Perth's tragic story left me deeply impacted. I clearly saw that so much more needed to be done on the ground in Indonesia and in the wild for the orangutans. I knew that their natural habitat was being destroyed at an alarming rate and I had seen, first hand, the cruel and heartless treatment they encountered at the hands of humans. But perhaps most importantly, I began to ask myself the question, "*What more could I do to help them?*"

A Chance Meeting with Chantek...

At the other end of the spectrum from the wild born orangutans which I came across in my work, were the captive born orangutans. These beings were held within zoos and primate research facilities across the globe in both developing and so called first world countries. You could be forgiven for assuming that at least the welfare and care of these orangutans would certainly have been of a much higher and more humane standard. However, in many cases, with the exception of the orangutans at Perth Zoo and a few other enlightened zoos dotted around the world, I found this assumption to be far from true. Because I was coming to understand that, for a being as intelligent and aware as an orangutan, captivity could be as painful and inflict just as much suffering upon them. This brings me to my chance meeting with Chantek.

During my work with the breeding program with the orangutans at Perth Zoo in 1997, I was asked to look for a new male orangutan to join our existing group. This was because all of the males born at Perth Zoo were obviously related to the females, as they were their offspring. So basically the community had grown into one large interconnected family. Therefore, there was a need to expand the gene pool within the group via the introduction of a new, healthy unrelated male.

In my search for this new addition, I had been able to locate and identify two male orangutans in the USA who were the right genetic match for our females. So I took a flight out to the USA to have a look at these two males as possible additions to the Perth orangutan community. One of these males was named Solok and he lived in a primate centre, situated just outside of Atlanta Georgia.

Now let's just say that this primate centre had a reputation within the industry as being a pretty horrible place for the primates it housed...and that was putting it mildly. This was because it was known as a place where vivisection experiments were conducted upon the primates on a regular basis.

Vivisection literally meaning: "*the cutting of or operation on a living animal usually for physiological or pathological investigation.*" [1]

These include, but are not limited to, surgeries, infecting them with diseases, administering drugs, poisoning for toxicity testing, brain research and using any other number of painful and inhumane procedures over time. Basically the organisation was conducting sanctioned and large scale animal torture by exposing the primates it had in its care, to a range of ongoing experiments and tests, all in the name of science.

For example, at the time that I was visiting the centre to meet and assess Solok, I was told by my guide that they were conducting an experiment which involved forcing the resident chimpanzees to smoke crack cocaine on a regular basis. The intention of this experiment was to assess the effects of using the drug on them and their babies. Their reasoning being that, as a 99% genetic match with us, the chimpanzees were a close analogue for studying the effects on the babies of human female crack cocaine addicts.

To my way of thinking, this was not only an appalling misuse of position and power on behalf of the organisation, but an outright case of animal cruelty and abuse. I was personally dumbfounded when the technicians explained to me what they were doing in the name of research. Quite frankly, it is times like these, when I come face to face with the human ignorance and brutality which sanctions this type of behaviour, that serve to reinforce my commitment to gaining greater compassion and respect for Great Apes. And at a wider level, to end all manner of animal suffering across the planet.

Perhaps an interesting thing to point out here is that, I could also see that the technicians who worked there were deeply affected by the procedures which they were expected to carry out on the primates. Whilst, they may not have recognised it within themselves, nor been aware of it at the time, I could see that they too suffered. As it is a well-known fact that the humans who have to physically execute cruel or torturous acts upon animals are also victims of the systems in which they work. In that, workers at abattoirs are more likely to have drug addictions, psychological issues, depression, and emotional problems than those who are not subjected to these brutalising environments. This is because these jobs and the tasks they entail greatly impact the human psyche at an innate level. The truth is that they run contrary to our own inner knowing of what is fair and just treatment of our fellow beings. Therefore they are intrinsically damaging and destructive places for both the humans and the animals who have the misfortune of finding themselves there.

Of course, centres like these are not open to the public and remain well hidden behind closed doors, so most of us are unaware of what's actually going on in the name of the research carried out on our behalf. And the only reason that someone like me was allowed inside the centre in the first place and able to see its workings, was because they no longer wanted Solok. In fact they were keen to move him on.

When I was taken to assess Solok, I found him held in one of a series of concrete bunker-like 6 x 6 foot cages. Each had metal bars at the front and an attached night sleeping quarters to the rear of the cage. As I walked towards Solok's cage, out of the corner of my eye I glimpsed some movement in the cage next door. Turning my head to look towards the distraction, my attention was caught by the sight of a larger and extremely overweight male orangutan coming out of his night quarters. This orangutan was so obese that as he moved towards the front of his cage, I couldn't actually see if he was using his back legs to walk with, or if he was literally having to drag himself across the floor due to his huge underbelly. It was a shocking sight to behold. In fact I'd never seen anything like it before, because healthy orangutans do not naturally carry very much extra weight, even in captivity.

However what immediately focussed my attention towards this orangutan was that as he approached, I realised that he was gesturing with his hands and fingers in an attempt to communicate with me. Even though I don't know how to read American sign-language, I suddenly twigged that he was actually using this form of signing to communicate with me as a fellow being. In complete surprise, I turned and asked the technician what this orangutan was trying to *say*. The technician looked blankly back at me and told me that he didn't know as no one had taken the time to learn sign language. However, he did tell me that this orangutan was named Chantek, and I instantly realised who was standing in this cage in front of me.

I had heard of Chantek many years ago and amongst the students of the Great Apes, he was almost a celebrity. In fact, this being was none other than the world famous orangutan who had been taught sign language in the 1970s. Originally born in captivity, at the age of nine months, Chantek had been transferred to the care of respected anthropologist and University of Tennessee at Chattanooga (UTC) professor, Dr Lyn Miles. For the next nine years of his life Chantek was raised and cared for by Dr Miles and her team much like a human child. He was taught sign language, chores and a simple form of exchange, and even attended university classes on campus. However, as Chantek approached his adolescent years and grew larger and stronger, there were fears that he may become unmanageable and a danger to his fellow students. At this point the difficult decision was made to return him to the primate centre. [2]

Therefore this incredibly intelligent, much loved orangutan, accustomed to a high level of human contact and interaction was consigned to a 6 x 6 foot cage within the primate centre... for the next eleven years of his life. Probably just as sadly, he was no longer able to communicate directly with his human keepers as he once had. Understandably, Chantek had fallen into a depressed state and had gained a large amount of weight, much like a depressed human would in the same situation.

I was personally and professionally stunned by the circumstances in which I found both Chantek and Solok. And if it had been possible to take both of these orangutans back to Perth Zoo with me, there and then, I would have done so. But unfortunately, this wasn't the case. My task was specifically to assess and select a single male orangutan who was in a suitable psychological and physical state to join the orangutan community at Perth Zoo. Therefore I spent the time assessing Chantek and Solok and determined that, even in his depressed and obese condition, Chantek would be a great candidate for transfer to Perth Zoo. This was because I knew that with some appropriate care and attention from our team, we could rehabilitate Chantek back to full mental and physical health. Furthermore, he would not only make a wonderful addition to the colony, but also be able to demonstrate his capacity for language to the public, thus increasing connection, understanding and empathy for orangutans.

Therefore I put in a request for Chantek to become a part of the vibrant and thriving community of orangutans at Perth Zoo. With this complete, I felt optimistic and hopeful about the prospect of working for this remarkable orangutan. However, before leaving for Australia, I discussed my request for Chantek to come to Perth with the staff at Zoo Atlanta. Apparently they then told the zoo's director that I had found Chantek and of my plans to bring him to Perth. However, I can only surmise that a powerful sense of patriotism overcame him, because he was quoted as saying, "No way will Chantek go to Perth. He should come to Zoo Atlanta instead." As the facility was within the same state and only a short journey from the primate centre, this was seen as a great option. Chantek was finally transferred to this zoo later in 1997, where he still resides to this day.

For me, although disappointed that we would not have the opportunity to work for him, at least Chantek was now housed in a more humane and engaging environment. Importantly, he was also able to continue his sign language training and show the public how special and intelligent orangutans are. Zoo Atlanta also offered him greater space to move around freely and keepers who once again engaged with him on a regular basis….so I was relieved on his behalf. However I was greatly disturbed by what I had seen of the conditions in which captive orangutans could be held and the ongoing suffering which they experienced under these circumstances.

And what of the message that Chantek had tried to express to me when we first met…what was it that he was trying to say? I later learned that whenever Chantek encountered a person he thought was a caretaker, he would consistently use his sign language skills to ask them to, *"Get the car keys and take him home."* [3]

Ultimately, neither of the two male candidates I assessed in the USA was transferred to Perth Zoo. Instead, we later secured a handsome male named Dinar from Toronto Zoo to join our Western Australian orangutan community.

The Orangutan Project Was Born…

Following my meeting with Chantek in 1997, I received the devastating news of Perth's injuries in the wild during his encounter with the illegal loggers. Within me something shifted. I felt a deep sense of responsibility and an urgent inner desire to do more for my orangutan friends…to somehow change their lives for the better wherever they were. In addition to this, I was no longer prepared to sit back and silently witness the wholesale destruction of their habitat, the cruel mistreatment and needless slaughter of these majestic beings and to mutely do nothing as they headed towards an inevitable, yet completely avoidable extinction.

I had finally come to a number of inescapable conclusions:

- Firstly, that all orangutans, no matter their circumstances, deserved *Compassion, Protection and Freedom.*
- Secondly, that alone, I could make a difference, but only a small one at best. However with a committed, focussed team, a co-ordinated organisation and a group of like-minded supporters along-side us, we could make a large scale impact on an ongoing basis.
- Thirdly, that there was no time to waste and the orangutans needed our help and assistance sooner, rather than later. It was time to act and that time was *Now.*

It was at this point that I became galvanised into action.

The Orangutan Project was born in late 1998 and has been consistently working towards improving the welfare and ensuring the survival of all orangutans ever since.

SECTION 1

MY JOURNEY TO ORANGUTANS

*"It's your road and yours alone. Others may walk
it with you but no one can walk it for you."*
Rumi

CHAPTER 1
A FASCINATION WITH ALL LIFE

"The privilege of a lifetime is being who you are."
Joseph Campbell

Much has been said about the impact our early childhood experiences have upon us as we mature into adulthood, specifically those in our formative first couple of years and up until around the age of seven. Amongst geneticists, neuro scientists, anthropologists and psychologists the debate typically focuses on the age old question of which holds the most influence in our development...

Is it Nature or Nurture, Genetics or Environment which hold the key?

Some researchers contend that it is primarily our natural genetic make-up which determines our future life as an adult. Whilst others support the argument that it is our early childhood environment and the *presence or absence of nurture* during this time, which carries the greatest weight in later life. However, The Dunedin Study, a landmark New Zealand based, longitudinal research project has been measuring the effects of early childhood experiences across a 1,000 strong participant base for over 40 years. In addition to this, it has also extensively researched the impact of natural genetic factors within its subjects and the adult lives they lead as a result.

Amongst their fascinating and ground breaking findings, all indicators suggest that from as young as two to four years of age, there are clear genetic and behavioural predictors within children which show how they will fare later on in life. Furthermore, this study has solid evidence that it is a combination of *both* our genetic predispositions and our early childhood experiences which have far reaching effects upon our mental and physical wellbeing, inner happiness and ability to successfully navigate the human experience. In fact it appears that these key factors work in *tandem* to create predictable outcomes for us far into the future.

For example, the study has identified two separate genes each which predispose those who are born with them within their genetic make-up, to either being aggressively / criminally violent or depressive by nature. However, possession of these genes alone does not guarantee that these individuals will automatically display such behaviours. Interestingly, when combined with a happy and supportive upbringing, the people who possessed these genes were highly unlikely to exhibit these tendencies. On the other hand, if these same individuals were subjected to a difficult, abusive, unsupportive or unloving childhood, they would be almost guaranteed to display these behaviours during their teenage or adult years. [4]

So the answer appears to be that both Nature and Nurture, Genetics and our Foundational Environments determine how we respond and react to life and the challenges with which it presents us.

From experience I can wholeheartedly say that the same is certainly true for our orangutan cousins. Because I have seen otherwise healthy, strong infant orangutans, who have been deprived of their natural and intensely nurturing early years with their mothers, have their development greatly impacted in the negative. In fact it can take years of rehabilitation to help them back to full physical and mental health. (This is something which I will be discussing in more detail in Section 2.)

For myself, as I reflect back over my early life and the path which led me to my work with my orange friends, I can clearly see where my natural, inborn inclinations and my learned approach to life were impacted by both my childhood experiences and my familial genetic background. Because, in many ways, there were specific choices which my parents made which either, nurtured and enhanced my instinctive nature, and those which instilled new and culturally based behaviours within my psyche.

Nurture-The Human Side of Things...

My initial start in life was what could only be termed as being relatively unremarkable and quite in keeping with the average middle class upbringing in 1960's Australia. Born in suburban Sydney in 1964 to Australian parents Bob and Glenda, I joined my older sister, Angel, as the second and youngest child to complete our family of four. My father, a fifth generation Australian Sydney-sider, had a rising career in the rapidly expanding field of advertising. My mother, a fourth generation Australian from country Queensland, was a fulltime home maker. She whole heartedly focussed her attention on raising Angel and I, providing us with a loving and caring upbringing and keeping the home running smoothly and seamlessly as possible. So together my parents ensured we were a stable and cohesive family unit living the typical suburban Aussie dream.

However, this was to change when I was around 18 months old and my father was given the opportunity to take up a transfer to his company's Hong Kong office. My young, upwardly mobile parents welcomed the chance to live and work in such an exotic and intriguing location and soon our family was on its way to this new adventure. It's important to remember that at the time Hong Kong was still a crown colony under British rule which meant that it was a melting pot of nationalities and an exciting frontier where Asian culture met western colonialism. So immediately our family, straight from the suburbs in predominantly white middle class Australia, became immersed in the vibrant, bustling, multi-cultural environment of 1960s Hong Kong. It was here we would stay until I was 15 years of age.

We settled into an area named Mount Davis, in the south west region of the island. Our new home was an apartment in a high rise development set amongst a cluster of other similar high rise apartment towers. Our new friends and neighbours were a mix of Chinese, Indians, British and Europeans. Angel's and my new playgrounds were either, the nearby carparks and streets surrounding our apartment building or the seemingly massive peak of Mount Davis which loomed over the landscape at around 260m in height. Even as youngsters we would head out to play with the many children living in the neighbouring apartments and form ourselves into competing soccer or baseball teams to while away the long, steamy days. Or if we felt particularly adventurous, we would make the arduous trek up to the top of Mount Davis itself. There we found the old abandoned British fortifications from years earlier which had been used by the British to defend Hong Kong from Japanese invasion forces. It was a fascinating place and we would play for hours in the overgrown old fortress bunkers and gun battlements with majestic, panoramic views across the water and surrounding islands below.

Seeing No Difference Between People...

Perhaps one of the earliest memories I have from our time in Hong Kong, was some time after we arrived. As a naturally inquisitive and curious child, I enjoyed listening to my parents' conversations and to being able to ask them questions as they arose in my mind. On this occasion, I had overheard Mum speaking with Dad about her interactions with some Chinese people at the local markets. This wasn't the first time that I had heard them mention "the Chinese" in their discussions, so this had obviously aroused my curiosity at the time. Here, I clearly recall innocently saying, "*When are we going to meet these Chinese people Mum?*"

Of course the truth was that I was surrounded by Chinese people and had already been interacting and playing with the local Chinese kids in my neighbourhood since we'd arrived. I just didn't know that they were *Chinese* as no one had ever officially introduced them to me as such. To my young mind I thought that they were people and I didn't see them *as other or different from me.* In fact it made little sense to me to focus upon the minor differences between us because my Chinese friends were simply kids to play with.

I think for most children this is the case as young minds are naturally more open and inclusive to beings from different races and cultures, because they see the similarities, rather than the differences between us. Fortunately for me, my parents encouraged this way of thinking and relating to people. And my life experiences in the cosmopolitan and multi-cultural environment of Hong Kong only served to reinforce this inclusiveness.

Thinking Across Cultures...

Before long, I was attending the city's Island School which was a mini melting pot of nationalities and diverse cultures. Once I had begun my schooling and began expanding my friendships, I developed two quite distinct, but equally fascinating groups of friends. Firstly I had made many firm friends within my neighbourhood and happily mixed with the collection of Chinese, Indians, Eurasians and British who lived in and around the flats. At school I had another group of friends from across the globe and together we experienced the unique and often surprising aspects of the city in which we lived. Without a doubt, growing up in the cosmopolitan environment of Hong Kong not only exposed me to different cultures, it also nurtured within me an enduring love and respect for all peoples.

At the same time as we were living in Hong Kong, in the mid-1960s to mid-1970s, came the meteoric rise to fame of one of the city's most famous sons...Bruce Lee. As a skilled practitioner and proponent of martial arts, actor, philosopher and outspoken modern day thinker, Bruce Lee captured the young minds and hearts of all Hong Kongese boys. I was no exception. With his mix of both American and Asian upbringing – he was actually born in San Francisco and raised in Kowloon- Bruce Lee's approach to life was a fascinating combination of western bravado and eastern wisdom. We loved his portrayals in his fast and furious martial arts movies. With Bruce Lee as our hero, we practiced our own version of Lee's *Jeet Kune Do* style of martial arts on each other and absorbed his philosophical approach to life.

Later, when the landmark television series, Kung Fu, was released in 1972 starring American actor David Carradine, I remember being similarly captivated. The series followed the story of a young half Chinese, half American man named Kwai Chang Caine who had been trained as a Shaolin monk before he left China. Each episode would focus on a new adventure as he wandered through the wild west of America in the late 1800's, on his journey to find his American father and half-brother. With his intense physical and spiritual training in the ways of Shaolin, Caine always tried to avoid conflict and attention. However because of his internal sense of integrity and responsibility, he would invariably be drawn into conflict and be forced to fight for justice to protect the innocent and down trodden in the lawless towns of the west. Of course my friends and I began to add Kung Fu to our repertoire of martial arts practice as we staged play fights between the goodies and the baddies in our neighbourhood playgrounds.

As young boys looking for hero figures to emulate, I think both Bruce Lee and the character Kwai Chang Caine epitomised all that was positive, wise and masterful within a strong male role model. They were men of discipline and philosophical understanding, yet were able to conquer most foes with their speed, agility and fighting skills. However, they practiced a defensive style of martial arts which meant that instead of seeking out or initiating conflict with others, they would only defend against an attack and usually on behalf of those who were unable to protect themselves. Perhaps, this way of thinking stayed with me into adulthood, as ultimately, this philosophy underpins my work with the orangutans to this day. To speak up for those who can't and to protect and defend those in need.

Nature-The Animal Side of Things...

Alongside my curiosity when it came to humans and their behaviours, I have always had a fascination with the natural world. This includes an innate wonder about the animals and the natural environments with which we share this beautiful planet we call home. For a long time, I used to think that this type of over-riding, animal loving, tree hugging appreciation was limited to only a small handful of environmentalists or *greenies*, as I've often been called. But I was wrong, because I have since come to learn that this type of in-born connection with all life, not only has a name, but is common to almost all human beings from birth...

It is called *biophilia* and, according to a number of great thinkers, from Aristotle to Erich Fromm, it literally means; "*a love of life and the living world.*" [5]

More recently, in his 1984 book, *Biophilia*, well known biologist and theorist, Edward O. Wilson, extended this definition of biophilia to encompass:

"*An innate and genetically determined affinity of human beings with the natural world...the urge to affiliate with other forms of life*" [6]

For me, this pretty much summed up and explained my life-long love of animals. In many ways it was a relief, because I had always been a little uncomfortable with the clichéd image of the animal loving environmentalist. Most importantly, I was intrigued by the fact that we as humans, are all born with this innate love of animals. Furthermore it was obvious that it is only through the learned, environmental impacts of cultural norms, religious ideology, economic priorities and business interests that we distance ourselves from animals and lose our instinctive affinity with the natural world. So it seems that we actually teach children to separate themselves from their connection with animals in order to justify our poor treatment and abuse of them. This was an inescapable and disturbing truth for me. However, as I grew up, I was fortunate enough to have parents who not only encouraged but also nurtured this part of me.

Obviously, because we lived in a high rise apartment in Hong Kong, I wasn't able to have a dog or large pets as a child. However, that certainly didn't stop me from having a colourful private menagerie of small and more apartment friendly animals in my bedroom from a young age. These included animals such as budgies, terrapins, tropical fish, gold fish, turtles and two cats. As you can imagine, I loved my animal friends and would spend hours playing with or observing them whenever I could. Interestingly, animals also seemed to like and respond to me too.

In addition to the animals I had at home, I was enthralled to see that the local communities and city streets of Hong Kong were also filled with an amazing array of exotic animals.

Firstly there were the bustling, crowded local food markets where you could find a vast range of animals in various stages of being dead and alive. Where live pigs, chickens, ducks, frogs, fish, crustaceans and even insects were bought and sold amongst a selection of meats, various animal body parts and other typically Asian fresh produce. It was an assault on all of the five senses to visit these lively trading places and it was where I saw many of the more interesting and diverse components of the local diet. But to the Hong

Kongese, this close involvement with the life and death of animals was part of everyday life.

As well as being exposed to the ever changing range of animals in the street markets, I also came into contact with some of the astonishing collection of wildlife which Hong Kong residents kept as pets. Back in those days, there were no laws against having a large or exotic animal as a pet. Furthermore, there was no protection for the animals from humans' desire to cage and *own* them. Perhaps this was because there was so much remaining natural forest and a seemingly unending supply of wildlife that no one ever imagined or even stopped to think that the animals were not an unlimited resource? However, as a result, unfortunately, wildlife was literally treated as a commodity and in any way humans saw fit. Basically because it didn't occur to anyone that there was an animal welfare issue at hand, or that this demonstrated a lack of compassion for these living beings.

Monkeys, Tigers and Bears…

Even today in many parts of Asia and Indonesia it is still commonplace to find within the local villages and urban communities, what could be termed as, *the village monkey.* These monkeys, gibbons and smaller primates are either caged, tethered or tied up somewhere in public and are literally known as the village pet. Primate pets were not uncommon in Hong Kong at the time. Even to the degree that kids often came to school with monkeys, and I recall seeing many such caged animals in and around the city. Even members of the ex-patriot community got into the habit of keeping them as pets whilst they lived in the region.

For example, I remember when I was around seven years old, Dad had made some friends amongst the expats he worked with at the time. As the story goes, Dad had casually mentioned to his friend that he liked his pet Capuchin monkey whilst at a social gathering at this man's home. Unbeknownst to Dad, his friend had interpreted his comment of *"I like your monkey"* to mean *"I would like to have your monkey."* So when it was time for his friend to leave Hong Kong and move back to his own country, he turned up at our apartment one weekend with the monkey in tow, as a parting gift for Dad.

Taken by surprise, Dad, somewhat reluctantly took possession of the monkey. Being a young animal lover, I was overjoyed at the idea of having this cute and intelligent little guy as part of our home. However the poor monkey had different ideas and was terrified by this turn of events. So much so, that it decided to attach itself to Dad's neck, desperately clinging to the spot, and would not let my father go. And no level of coaxing, negotiating, food treats or careful prying off of the monkey's small hands, made any difference to the situation. So Dad literally had to walk around the apartment with the monkey attached to his neck. At night he even had to go to bed and sleep with it there because it refused to budge from its position of relative safety.

Understandably, it got a bit much for my father. Faced with the proposition that he would have to go to work with the monkey still attached to his neck, he made the decision that the monkey needed to go to a new and more suitable home. So he contacted his friend, and as politely as possible, asked him to come and retrieve the animal before he left the country. Whilst my parents were greatly relieved when the friend arrived to remove the monkey, I was very disappointed that I couldn't keep this new primate friend.

I also remember another time when our family was visiting Singapore for a vacation break. I saw that there was a gibbon tied to the children's play equipment at the back of the apartments where we were staying. My dad and I went down to the playground to see the gibbon and we found this poor little being tethered to the monkey bars, unable to escape, exposed to the elements and whatever may come its way. Dad went over to check that it was OK and played with the gibbon for a while. Sadly, even though I asked, Dad wouldn't let me get too close to the gibbon because he thought that it may have been a little too unpredictable for me to handle safely.

It was also not unheard of for some residents in Hong Kong to own and house a tiger. As young cubs, they could be kept in the home as pets, however as the animals grew older and stronger, the option of keeping a wild, mature tiger in the family residence was obviously out of the question. So this meant a different solution was needed and usually, this would result in the animal being kept captive in a cage on the roof of the apartment block where the *owners* lived. So once in this unenviable position the tiger remained caged on a roof high above the ground and far removed from its jungle habitat, because it was not the sort of animal which could be put on a leash and taken for a walk around the block.

Why would someone keep a tiger as a pet, you may ask? I think it was mainly for the prestige of owning such a strong, powerfully beautiful animal and probably just because they could. The thinking at the time was that they wanted a tiger, they could get one, so they caged it, fed it and kept it as a pet…no further questions were asked. Unfortunately, the ethics and morality of keeping a large predator in these circumstances didn't seem to enter anyone's mind.

I'll also never forget our trips to the local beach at sunset during the warmer months where we would sometimes swim and play in the cooling waves as a way of escaping the sweltering Hong Kong heat. Animals were allowed onto the beaches then, so it wasn't unusual to see many pets being brought down to the water by their owners. However, on one occasion as we were walking down to the water, I looked along the beach and was amazed to see two large bears, one brown and one black, bounding exuberantly and freely across the sand at the water's edge. Running alongside them was their *owner*, a local resident who was calling to the bears and playing with them as they splashed around in the surf. Apparently in summer this was a regular sight as the man brought his bears down to the ocean in the back of his van to have a run and cool off in the water. Afterwards he would round them up and take them back home to their cage at his house. As a young boy, I was understandably entranced by the sight of the bears on the beach and sometimes encountered them when we had our swims.

The American Passenger Pidgeon...

By the 1960s and 1970s there were some fantastic television programs dedicated to exploring the natural world, including National Geographic and the famous Ocean Explorer documentaries of Jacques Cousteau. Always fascinated by nature, I watched these programs whenever I could, either by myself or with the family. And it was around this time that I remember watching one such television nature documentary on the rapid mass extinction of the American Passenger Pidgeon. It was a documentary which profoundly affected me.

On this occasion, I was watching some local Hong Kong programming on television and a documentary on the sad end to the Passenger Pidgeon came on to the screen. Riveted by the story and amazed at how an animal which had been numbered at over 130 million breeding adults in 1871 and also known as the most abundant bird population in North America, perhaps even the world, could end its time on Earth as a species by 1914.

Apparently this pigeon was legendary for its massed migratory flocks of literally millions upon millions of individual birds flying in unison across vast areas of the American mainland. Their flocks were reputed to be so massive that it could take hours for a single group of the birds to pass over a location. In fact, the course of their flight could literally block out the sun from the sight of those below lucky enough to witness the phenomenon. In nature, their enormous flocks were their protection, however, when it came time for them to face the threat of the newly arrived European human predator, this characteristic led to their ultimate downfall. Their massed flocks made them exceptionally easy targets for the nets, guns, poisons, use of fire and trapping practices of the American settlers. So sadly, a bird which had lived in harmony and thrived alongside the Native American Indians for thousands of years, was ruthlessly hunted into extinction within a few short decades. And this beautiful force of nature disappeared from the face of the earth forever. [7]

However, I think the scenes which impacted me the most, were in the closing minutes of this documentary. It was here that it ended with a focus on the last American Passenger Pigeon to die. Her name was Martha and she lived alone in Cincinnati Zoo as the sole survivor of her species. Martha died in captivity at the age of 29 in 1914.

I was overwhelmed with a profound sense of loneliness and despair at the thought of how this last pigeon must have felt to be forever alone, with no prospect of being saved. I was haunted by this story as a child and today still feel a deep sense of regret over the lack of awareness which humanity exhibited. One which made them unable to see that they were responsible for the extinction of such an abundant species as the American Passenger Pidgeon. This cautionary tale happened only just over a century ago, yet still to this day it appears that we haven't learned much over this time. Even now, humans are still responsible for recklessly bringing so many other species to the brink of extinction... including the Sumatran and Bornean orangutans.

Ocean Park Hong Kong...

Finally, perhaps as a sign of things to come for me, another of the regular experiences I had with animals whilst I lived in Hong Kong, were the special times I spent going to Ocean Park Hong Kong. This was well known in the region as a Marine Mammal Park, Oceanarium, Zoo and Animal Theme Park situated in the Southern District of Hong Kong. I used to go there quite a bit because I loved to see the animals and it was also relatively close to where we lived. I would wander around the exhibits and try to catch a glimpse of all of the animals being active within their enclosures and it was here that I first formed my childhood dream of working with animals.

I clearly remember one day when I was around the age of 13, and on one of my many visits to the park, I observed a zoo keeper quietly going about his work. He seemed happy and relaxed and it struck me that he was not only able to work in the outdoors, get close to the animals, but he was also wearing gumboots! It was at that moment that I recall thinking to myself how wonderful it must be to be able to work with animals and wear gumboots all day. It must be close to heaven, I imagined. I never forgot this thought and the idea of working at a zoo stayed with me for years into my future.

Therefore, my early, formative childhood years were a solid combination of both nature and nurture. My parents gave me a secure and loving family life as a foundation from which to grow. They exposed me to a diverse and exotic culture during our time living in Hong Kong and encouraged my natural curiosity for people and new ideas. Alongside this, they nurtured and expanded my instinctive love of animals and allowed me to experience the joy of caring for and raising my own menagerie of pets. Interestingly, even though my parents loved animals, they were like most westerners in their views about the *rights of animals*. In that, they liked cats, dogs, birds, fish and the other animals we deem as pets, but there was a-disconnect between these and so called livestock meat or agricultural animals. Meaning that I grew up eating meat and being blind to the suffering that these animals experienced for the sake of our accepted dietary choices.

However, by this stage within me were perhaps the first inklings of a deep compassion for all living beings and the direction my life would take. Because I know, without a doubt, that these basic ways of seeing the world have greatly impacted the choices I've made and the path I've taken along the way. This was to become clearer as my family made the move back to the sunny shores of Australia.

CHAPTER 2
LEARNING TO LEARN, MY OWN WAY

"I'm not teaching you anything, I just help you to explore yourself."
Bruce Lee

I am a strong believer in the intrinsic value of education and ongoing learning. However, as a child and later as a growing teenage boy, traditional school based education just didn't work for me. In fact, for most of my time at Island School in Hong Kong, I was what was then termed as a *low-performer*. I was regularly at the bottom of my class in most subjects and had never read a book fully until after I left the school system. However, the funny thing was I knew within myself that I wasn't actually a stupid child. To me it just appeared that the mainstream education system didn't cater for my type of intelligence.

I finally came to the conclusion that I didn't like the way my education was going and I definitely didn't want to continue to fail at school. So I decided to change this situation. Firstly I knew that all individuals were intelligent in different ways and each of us had our own natural processes for making sense of the world. More importantly, I knew myself. I understood that I was not good at simply remembering data, dates and seemingly unrelated or irrelevant facts and parroting them back in tests. On the other hand, I saw myself as a logical, clear thinker and knew that once I understood concepts, formulae or key pieces of information and how these related to each other, I just *got things*. I also had relatively good problem solving and solution seeking skills, so I sat down and devised my own learning system to improve my results.

To do this, I went through all of my school work and put everything that I thought was of importance onto small cards. Using these cards on a regular basis, I then memorised everything I needed to know for each subject as part of my new learning plan. Even enrolling my mother to help me with regular quizzes. Suddenly my school marks and grades began to steadily improve, and within six months, I went from the bottom of the class in some of my subjects, to the top. I began to excel in Science, the Humanities and Art and I even started to enjoy the process of learning as everything began to make *sense* for me. Even though I was experiencing a new level of success in these subjects, it still didn't mean that I would complete and submit my homework. And I can remember spending the first 15 minutes or so of my classes stuck outside in the corridor as my frustrated teachers punished me for not completing my homework. I was also never going to excel in English and English Literature, but I could live with that.

However, I was able to prove to myself and demonstrate to my teachers that, even though the vast majority of kids can fit into mainstream education, the truth was I did not fall into that category. So in many ways, as schooling did not cater for my type of intelligence, I gained my education, *in spite of the system*, not because of it. What I also realised was that I had the intelligence to understand how the academic system worked and had used this to operate within it to suit myself. This was an important lesson for me and one which I would take forward into my time at University and ultimately during my life working for animals. This quote from Albert Einstein pretty well sums up my thoughts on intelligence and learning:

"Everybody is a genius. But if you judge a fish by its ability to climb a tree then it will live its whole life believing that it is stupid."
Albert Einstein

Around this time I also remember being given a vocational aptitude test. In the ensuing one-on-one interview to discuss my results, I told the teacher that I wanted to become a zookeeper. After looking at my score the teacher proceeded to talk me out of the idea. Ultimately he finished his argument for me to forget this childhood dream, with the fact that zookeeper jobs were mostly lifetime positions which only came up rarely. So it would be highly unlikely I would ever be able to gain such a job. At the time, I reluctantly gave up on this dream. I was 14 years old and I was just about to experience a steep learning curve in many areas of my life.

At age 15, instead of going home to Sydney, my parents chose to leave Hong Kong and settle the family on the west coast of Australia in Perth. Here I found myself in the southern suburbs of 1970s Perth. A city known as one of the most remote in the world. I must say it was certainly a shock to my system in terms of culture, diversity and size. Unlike the bustling, somewhat chaotic, multi-cultural neighbourhoods around our apartment block in Hong Kong, our new family home in suburban Bull Creek seemed lacking in vibrancy and character. Instead of the high rises and ocean surrounds of my Asian home, we lived in a quiet, housing sub division in predominantly white, middle class Western Australia. I definitely had some internal adjusting to do, because suddenly life felt flat and my new, quarter *acre home and land packaged* environment, a little bland.

To add to this marked shift in our surroundings, I was soon enrolled into the local school in the area, Rossmoyne Senior High School. Immediately I experienced a different type of approach to education. This was because Rossmoyne SHS turned out to be a *super school* which meant it was possibly the closest a state school could get to operating like a private school. It prided itself upon the academic and sporting performance of its students and was relatively strict about the behaviour and attitudes of all who attended. Not only did the staff and teachers of Rossmoyne SHS have certain expectations of their students, they were also very clear that even if you weren't a natural academic, everyone had to at least give their best effort.

Learning to Earn...

At the same time as I was making some changes within my academic life, I also knew that it was time for me to start generating my own income. Quite simply, I needed the money because I was becoming increasingly interested in another passion of mine, motorbikes and classic cars. In order to be able to save up for and ultimately buy my dream car, I knew I needed to get a job. Fortunately, there was a local fast food franchise, called *Red Rooster*. Red Rooster was an Australian based chicken outlet with a number of stores in the area. Thus I started my illustrious working career as a lowly paid, part time kitchen hand at $3.36 an hour. I spent my time there working behind the scenes to process, produce and package a range of fast, cheap and supposedly delicious, boxed chicken and chip meals.

As a part of the kitchen hand team, our morning set up work entailed de necking and stuffing multiple crates of frozen whole chicken carcasses, putting them onto long rotisserie rods and then basting them with fat as they roasted in the specially made ovens. Once the chickens were cooked, we were ready for service and were required to cook the additional chips, vegies and gravy which accompanied most of the meals. It was surprisingly physically demanding work, especially when the lunch or dinner time rushes were on, and in the kitchen we all worked hard to make sure that the meals came out hot, tasty and fast. Typically our weekend shifts started at 8.00 am and went through to the late afternoon around 5.00pm. I would do the Friday night as well as the Saturday and Sunday weekend day shifts, just to earn more money towards my ultimate aim of buying my own car. Because, as a car crazy teenager, I was on a mission and nothing would stop me.

Due to the nature of fast food chain stores, they necessarily relied upon teenage and student labour as we were classified as *junior staff* and therefore only attracted the correspondingly small junior-hourly-rates of pay. However, the good thing about this was that our work team was generally made up of teenagers from the local area so we got to work alongside each other and were able to create a unique sense of comradery. This meant we often had some interesting conversations about life, the universe and everything as we worked amongst the roasted chicken and fried chips. Basically it made the time fly past and to this day I am still in contact with some of the friends I made at Red Rooster.

After focussing my efforts so dedicatedly towards my part time job, I am happy to say that I was financially self-sufficient at age 15. And even though I still lived at home rent free with Mum and Dad, I otherwise paid my way and managed my money accordingly. As a consequence, I was able to buy my own motor bike at age 15 for $350. Even better still, not long afterwards I purchased my first car for the princely sum of $450 at 16 years of age. Things seemed to be looking up for me.

Off to University...

Because I had been able to master a number of Tertiary Admittance Examination (TAE) subjects using my study system, I did well in my final exams for Biology, Physics, Maths and Art. As a result I was able to secure a place at the Western Australian Institute of Technology (WAIT- which would later become known as Curtin University). With my results being high enough to gain entrance to university level study for most streams of my choice it came down to whether I would pursue an arts course or follow the path of science.

Surprisingly, I had inherited a talent for art and drawing from my father's artistic family however, during my high school biology course, I had come to love the subject and was fascinated with the study of the natural environment. Combined with my childhood passion for animals and the fact that I hadn't quite given up on the idea of one day working with them, science ultimately won me over. So straight after leaving school in 1981, I enrolled into a three year Bachelor of Applied Science Degree, majoring in biology and specialising in zoology.

I commenced my degree in early 1982.

I wish I could say it was all clear sailing for me during my university degree. But even though I loved biology and zoology, I found the first couple of years of study particularly dull and uninspiring, to say the least. This was because the course was structured with more general and statistical study units in the early years and it was only in third year that things began to look remotely interesting. Again I did the minimum amount of study and often skipped lectures, preferring to do my own form of learning to get me through the exams. Basically I just scraped by with most units, except in subjects like physics where I was able to just turn up to exams and achieve around 80% in my final marks. So for the first couple of years, I did only the bare basics at university, whilst my life and world revolved around cars, friends and work.

On the career front I remained focussed upon my part time work at Red Rooster and managed to simultaneously hold down two different jobs at two separate stores. In addition to this, I spent some time in the Army Reserve's University Regiment for extra cash. At home, I was able to remain living with Mum and Dad, but had the pleasure of moving into a large shed at the rear of their property. This I turned into my own version of a cool bachelor pad which then doubled as a *first home* for both my first and second wives. I can honestly say that I happily lived in, what became known as, *Leif's shed* for many years of my life.

However, by the third year of university we actually began to study animals at a more in depth level and I also opted for some anthropology units. I was captivated by the complex theories of evolution and the development of human societies across the world. We also began to look at our ape-like ancestors, primates and the very clear genetic relationships between the Great Apes and human beings. At last I found that study for me had come alive. I was engaged and personally interested. Also thanks to an inspiring teacher, George Newland, no longer was my study based around just facts and figures. Instead it held a deeper meaning and its impact was that I felt I had finally found my forte. I was excited to learn and my mind was switched on.

In 1985 I graduated from Curtin University with a Bachelor of Applied Science Degree and was relatively satisfied with my efforts. Furthermore, I felt I had achieved the required level of insight and understanding of the natural world to qualify myself for a future working with my beloved animals. However, there was one small hitch, I was still working in the chicken fast food industry. And, as I kept getting fired from my jobs at Red Rooster, due to my now 21+ *senior age* and the higher wages they had to pay me, I had moved onto a manager's job at a rival company. So there I was, fresh out of university, working full time as a manager at Chicken Treat Hamilton Hill, another fast food chain in the area. It wasn't a great situation.

Unfortunately, this management position meant that I would have to start at around 8.00am, spend the whole day inside working and generally come home in the dark after closing hours at 10pm. My life began to blur into one long *early start, late finish* and I began to count the days until my rostered two days off per week. In addition to this, I also started to experience a Mondayitis type of stress and anxiety at the thought of going back to work after my weekend. It was as if I was caught in a kind of waking nightmare. I realised that I was not suited to working in this monotonous indoor environment, away from the sun, the seasons, fresh air and animals, and I was desperately unhappy. I just knew that there had to be something better out there for me.

Finally, I became so disheartened at the thought of returning to work during one of my days off, that I decided to write to the Perth Zoo. In my letter to them I asked if they would consider me for any future positions with the zoo. My approach was totally out of the blue and I wasn't even applying to fill an existing job vacancy. I simply wanted to throw my hat into the ring and ask for an opportunity, as the zoo seemed to be the perfect place for me to work outdoors with animals. Basically I told them that I would do any kind of work if they would just give me a chance.

Two weeks later Perth Zoo called me in for a job interview.

In preparation, I read the official zoo marketing brochure, looked at the aims of the organisation and included some of these when answering questions during the interview. Apparently I blitzed it and they loved me. Within a week, I had secured a position as an entry level zoo keeper. I would finally be working with animals and I'd be wearing gumboots all day too! As my friends and colleagues always say, I am not an overly emotional person, however when I received this news I was ecstatic.

A Zoo Keeper at Last…

My career as a zoo keeper began just before my 22nd birthday, in September 1986. Believe me when I say that I started out pretty much on the bottom rung of the zoo keeper ladder. However, I was so excited to have my dream job, that this didn't worry me at all. In fact I almost revelled in the idea that I would work my way up through the ranks of the team, based upon my skill and care of the animals.

Another thing which I came to realise when I started working at the zoo was that, in many ways, the zoo management saw their employment of me as a kind of bold new experiment. This was because, as a university science graduate, I was seen as over qualified for the position of zoo keeper. As the strange truth was that I was the first ever Biology Degree holding keeper to be employed at Perth Zoo. Interestingly, now it is the norm to have zoo keepers on staff at major zoos, who are university educated. But back then, they put people into two separate camps, the first were seen as the *practical hands on animal type* of people and the second were considered to belong to the *stereotypical fumbling academic* who was intelligent, but not good in the field. They did not think that you could be physical, capable and intelligent all in the one package. So they took a chance when they gave me the job and I was keen to make sure their calculated risk paid off for them... and for me too.

I started off being placed in the Bird Section within the zoo for the simple reason that it was where the keeper's job was on offer... and this is where I stayed for the first 18 months or so of my time there. This meant that I worked closely with our feathered friends to feed them, clean their enclosures and care for their general welfare. In the main I enjoyed working for the birds however I found that as the vast majority of their behaviour was instinctive rather than consciously decided, my work with them was quite predictable and somewhat unchallenging. Therefore, with the exception of the ducks and penguins who later displayed great character and were quite interactive with the keepers, things at the Bird Section were pretty ho-hum and even boring for me.

However, whilst I was settling in to zoo working life and learning the ropes with the birds I also came to experience the fascinating and even surprising culture of another species at the zoo... the human keepers.

A Hunter Culture...

The first thing I noticed when I joined the ranks of the zoo keepers was that it was a very male dominated space. In fact, so much so that the sole female keeper on the team seemed to be made an honorary man, just so she didn't feel left out. Secondly the working environment was like something out of the wild-west, where we all had a relatively rough and tumble approach to our jobs and the animals within our care. Remember that this was a time well before the rules and regulations around Occupational Health and Safety, so we definitely took some risks on a weekly, if not daily basis. Lastly, in many ways, we were hunters. What I mean by this is that our behaviours were what could best be described as a *coalition of male chimps*. I specifically use the analogy of chimps here because they too gather in groups of males to go out to hunt, capture and even kill their prey. (I'll explain this point shortly)

For example, in the Bird Section when we had to capture an ostrich for a health check or enclosure transfer, we would chase them around the enclosures and catch them by the tail. Then two other keepers would grab their wings. Once under our control, we would then just walk them up to where they needed to be without further assistance. With some of the smaller and less dangerous animals we would often jump on them to catch them. Furthermore, I will never forget a couple of encounters I had when I was first learning how to care for the ungulates or hooved animals, such as cattle, zebras and goats...

At the time, I was still very new to the job and as an introduction to this section, I was given a zoo diet sheet for the ungulates and simply told to, "*Go and look after them.*" Not knowing anything about them or their particular herd-like behaviours, I innocently walked straight into the enclosure for the Banteng Cattle (a species of large horned cattle from South East Asia). Immediately as they saw me and smelt their food, they all charged towards me as one mass. The result being that I was literally picked up off my feet by them, and carried across the enclosure on their backs. It must have been a hilarious sight, but once they had stopped their forward charge, I had to carefully extricate myself from the enclosure. During the same time, I also went in to feed the camels and was chased straight out by the aggressive alpha male and felt I had to run for my life. It was a very rough and ready environment with little or no training, you just had to adapt and swim with the current...or sink.

On another occasion I witnessed a keeper perform a very gutsy thing in the face of certain peril. The keeper's name was Joe, and he and I were in the raceway – a protected walkway in between animal enclosures- separating some of the ungulate enclosures. Somehow a mob of stampeding Scimitar Oryx – a species of African Antelopes with extremely long pointed antlers- had gotten into the raceway and were charging straight towards us. Luckily for me, I was able to jump to safety by scrambling up the raceway fence. However Joe was an older man and had no time to respond physically. Instead he turned towards the stampede and stood his ground. I watched in amazement as he stood stock still, in the middle of the narrow raceway with his trusty rake in hand and commandingly yelled, "*Stop!*" at the charging animals. Surprisingly the lead animal halted in its tracks and the others immediately followed suit. Joe was left standing only feet away from the newly subdued Scimitar Oryx, narrowly averting his certain injury, if not death.

During times of animal escapes within the zoo – yes, animals escaped their enclosures quite regularly back then - we would all be called over to set up a hunting party to recapture the offending animal. In a strange way I think we relished these group hunting sessions as we tracked down the escapees. I noticed that we acted with an adrenaline fuelled pack mentality and were very effective in our joint aim of catching our quarry.

In particular, I recall getting quite skilled at catching Vervet monkeys as these intelligent little primates were serial escapees. At one time at the Perth Zoo, the Vervet monkeys were housed in a newly designed enclosure which was only escape proof in the mind of the architect. However, invariably they would make a run for it which meant they would head off the large lakes and submerge themselves underwater as they tried to sneak across the moat to the islands. We keepers would all be out with our nets looking for the monkeys as they surfaced, but I learnt that I could track them by the trail of bubbles reaching the water's surface as they travelled underneath it. Ultimately I would follow the air bubbles and be waiting with my net as the monkey approached. Basically, our hunts were a diversion in our schedules and became part of a good days' work at the zoo.

Finally there were our rat hunting incursions. Understandably, with all of the animals in captivity, their feed and the leftover food scraps and rubbish from the daily parade of human visitors, the zoo was a perfect place for rats. Added to this, Perth Zoo is situated in close proximity to the Swan River, which adds to the likelihood of rats in the area. So we regularly had a noticeable rat problem, which rat poisons alone could not curtail. Therefore, it was not uncommon, in the early days, for our group of male zoo keepers to be called up for a ritual rat hunt. This involved us forming into our hunting pack, arming ourselves with rubber hoses and heading off after our poor unsuspecting prey. I am not proud to say this, and I certainly don't condone our behaviour, but we would simply hit the rats over the head with our hoses to stun them and then proceed to quickly dispatch them with a swift death. I specifically recall that to do this as zoo keepers, generally people who loved animals, we had to switch off our feelings and become almost psychopaths. In this state we were highly effective hunters, but had no feeling involved in our actions. It was a strange phenomenon to observe in myself and my keeper friends, however very soon I would come to understand how the mind of a killer worked.

After about 18 months of time working with the Bird Section and learning the ropes as a keeper, I pleaded with zoo management to be moved off this area and transferred to some more interesting and challenging work. Shortly after this my wish was fulfilled and I was moved to the Carnivore Section. It was to provide me with an inside view into the lives of some natural born killers.

In With the Big Cat Carnivores…Lions, Tigers and Leopards

Joining the Carnivore Section meant that I was now going to be dealing with the Big Cats, such as tigers, lions and leopards on a daily basis. For me I immediately enjoyed the challenge and the change in pace that the care of the carnivores entailed. In fact, straight away I noticed a marked difference in the atmosphere of this section. This was because when dealing with the Big Cats, who are literally killing machines, there is always a distinct energy or electricity when you are in their presence. It just seems to hang in the air around them and from what people describe from a safari experience, this feeling is quite common. I just sensed that I would have to be on my guard with them and I saw, that as apex predators, the Big Cats were certainly less than predictable in their behaviour. This was a refreshing shift and in marked contrast to my time in the Bird Section.

I immediately took a liking to Alistair, the zoo's resident male lion. In many ways he behaved like a big boisterous dog. Still relatively young and raised in captivity he used to play and chase around his enclosure. He also loved having his belly scratched and I learned that as lions are the only truly social cat living in grouped lion prides, they are more easily capable of seeing humans as something other than prey. This meant that when dealing with them it was possible to perceive another dimension to their psyches. I also learned the chilling fact that due to their pride structure, lions often eat their prey alive, so in the wild they would eat you before killing you. Obviously within the zoo however, they were only fed meat from pre-slaughtered animals.

Another aspect which drew me towards Alistair was the fact that he initially had to be housed by himself, away from the females. Because as a young and inexperienced lion the lionesses used to beat him up if he was put with them. This was due to the fact that he was still too soft and too young to behave as the alpha male of the pride, which the females not only expected, but demanded of him. So we had to keep him separated from them until he was older, bigger and prepared to step up into his dominant role.

I was also able to get acquainted with the zoo's tigers, Delores and Anitra. Compared to the rough and bristle-like fur of the lions, the tigers' fur was silky, soft and luxurious. As natural born killers, tigers are known to be elusive and shy. Usually attacking their prey from behind and immediately killing them by snapping their necks before dragging the carcass off to be eaten in privacy and safety. In their jungle home, tigers naturally know to keep away from humans as much as possible as they recognise humans as dangerous predators. However, in the captive zoo setting, I was able to play tug of war with them using some rope which had been passed through the protective wire mesh of their enclosures.

Understandably, we rarely ventured into the tigers' enclosure, however we did have to go in once in a while when one of the animals was ill and not accessible from the boundary. Basically the procedure was to go in with a gun whilst the vet darted the tiger with a tranquiliser to subdue the animal before removing it for treatment. In one instance before guns were common place, the vet had darted the tiger and I was sent in to secure it on an inspection table in its night quarters, at the rear of its enclosure. However, unfortunately the vet hadn't given the tiger quite enough tranquiliser and as I went over to check that the tiger was safely on the examination table, he proceeded to sit up. At the same time the vet and nurse came into the area and seeing what had happened they panicked, ran out of the door and locked it behind them. So there I was, locked in the room, face to face with a large groggy tiger. I slowly had to negotiate my way out of the night-quarters by backing away from the half tranquilised carnivore whilst convincing the vet and nurse to quickly unlock the door... which thankfully, they did.

And then there was Fury the male leopard, and my experience with this leopard would forever change the way I saw the killer instinct.

I remember this incident occurred one day as I was walking along the raceway between two Big Cat enclosures. Fury was in an enclosure on one side with his female mate, a leopard named Princess. As I progressed along the raceway, I instinctively felt that I was being observed. Then in an instant, I saw a flash from the corner of my eye as Fury unexpectedly decided to launch himself across the enclosure with me firmly in his sights as his prey. At lightning speed he flew through the air towards me in a death pounce. However, in his killer state he had failed to remember that the enclosure's side fence acted as an impenetrable barrier between the two of us.

In that moment, I was shocked and frozen to the spot. Fury was only feet away from me, hanging on the wire mesh fence which separated me from certain death. By this stage I had come to know that leopards were fairly violent types of animals, but his attack had been thwarted and he couldn't get to me to kill me. Still in his instinctive killer state, he looked around his enclosure. Within a split second he had launched himself across the space, grabbed his mate Princess around the throat with his jaws and began suffocating her to death in front of me. I was stunned, but rushed around to the back of his enclosure in an attempt to scare him off Princess. With the help of some other keepers, we finally got him secured inside his night enclosure so we could get to Princess. But it was too late because he had already killed her.

I was in shock, but what I so very clearly remember from this momentary encounter with Fury, were his eyes…because they had changed in that moment of attack. In fact, for the whole day afterwards, when I looked at him I saw there was no soul, no consciousness within his eyes. They were dark, cold, and blank. I assume that this chilling characteristic is something akin to when a potential victim or survivor of a serial killer explains that, *"When he picked me up and I looked into his eyes I could see nothing there, there was no humanity."* Because that is what I saw in Fury's eyes that day. There was a dark ignorance and complete lack of awareness, compassion or recognition of me as another being. So from Fury's attack upon me and the death of Princess, his mate, I knew that I had witnessed a predator's lethal instinct. More than this, I had also seen into the eyes of a killer.

What I was able to appreciate about this incident was that carnivores are killers, even though they are *higher order* animals and seemingly have a greater awareness of others. However, nature doesn't evolve killing machines such as leopards, tigers and lions to then give them empathy or guilt over their actions. Because they are killers and have to be so in order to survive… it is just what they do. So the animal's awareness of others switches off as it goes into killer mode. Therefore it kills without sin in many ways, as it does so for food not pleasure, taste, convenience or solely for the hunt.

I spent around six to nine months with the carnivores and was able to learn much about their behaviours whilst with them. However, an unexpected turn of events was soon to bring me face to face with a group of beings who were to change the course of my life forever.

CHAPTER 3
MEETING MY GINGER-HAIRED MATCH

"...chimpanzees, bonobos, gorillas and orangutans are thinking,
self-aware beings capable of planning ahead, who form lasting social
bonds with others and have a rich social and emotional life.
The great apes are therefore an ideal case to show the
arbitrariness of the species boundary."

Peter Singer

After some changes in the staffing of the Primate Section and the retirement of the much loved and respected Head Primate Keeper, Charlie Broomfield, I was offered the opportunity to transfer across to this section in mid-1988. Of course, I jumped at the chance and very soon I found myself face to face with a wide array of primates from across the globe and in all shapes and sizes.

At that time the Primate Section at Perth Zoo had everything from gibbons, lemurs, tamarins, macaques, capuchins, baboons and monkeys right through to our closest cousins, the Great Apes, with chimpanzees, and orangutans. As much as I genuinely appreciated all of the beings within this section, I was naturally most drawn towards the shy, elusive and highly intelligent orangutans. Due to this initial attraction I was really looking forward to meeting the members of the world renowned colony of orangutans housed at the zoo and to working for them. By this stage the zoo's orangutan program was already recognised internationally as being a leader in the breeding of orangutans in captivity. Between the years of 1970 to 1993 there were

25 orangutan babies born at Perth Zoo. This in itself was a remarkable statistic for the zoo and I felt both excited and privileged to become part of the successful Primate Section Team.

Reg Gates, My Hippy Mentor...

As part of the Primate Section team, I was fortunate enough to work with both Reg Gates and Dr Rosemary Markham. As well as being a Dr of Philosophy with over 30 years of study into the behaviour of captive orangutans, Rosemary was also Charlie Broomfield's wife. Reg Gates was a Primate Section Keeper, and a man who was to have a major influence upon my life and my work for years to come. I can only describe Reg as a man of great compassion and dedication who loved the primates he worked for and who worked tirelessly for their welfare. A big, cuddly teddy bear of a man, Reg was also a self-confessed old hippy from Chicago, USA who had joined the Primate Section a year earlier. As my direct boss we hit it off straight away and I got to learn about him both as a conservationist and a friend.

One of the stories which Reg shared with me from his youth stood out as one which I never allowed him to live down. Better still, I think it best demonstrates his ability to laugh at himself and life in general. This was because as a young man living in Chicago in the 1960s he was a major fan of the progressive music scene at the time. As the story goes, one day in August 1969 some friends came over to see Reg and his first wife and invited them to join a group travelling to an upcoming music festival in New York State. After hearing about the plans for the festival, Reg turned down the invitation, saying that he thought the event would probably be a flop. So his friends went on their way and Reg stayed at home in Chicago with his wife. However, the festival which Reg missed out on turned out to be none other than the legendary, four day hippy love-in musical event called Woodstock.

With an audience of over 400,000 people and a performing line up of some of the most famous musicians of their time, the memory of Woodstock still lives on to this day. This was a majorly bad decision for any self-respecting 1960s hippy and I took great joy in reminding Reg of this fact during our time together.

However, along with his hippy tendencies, Reg was a role model for doing the right thing even when it wasn't personally convenient for him to do so, and for wanting to make the world a better place. Whilst working with him I witnessed the energy and passion with which he performed his job. He was always trying to improve the conditions and welfare of the primates in his care. Because of this he often ran into problems with a sometimes less than supportive zoo management team. In the early days Reg battled with this situation, but refused to give up hope for improving the situation for captive primates. He also began the charity organisation, The Silvery Gibbon Project, which still runs to this day and upon which I based so much of what would one day become The Orangutan Project. Needless to say, we became firm friends and in many ways we saw each other as comrades working alongside each other for a cause greater than ourselves. So, without a doubt, I was able to work and interact with some great people within the Primate Section. And, of course, there were the primates themselves.

Our Closest Relatives, the Great Apes....

During my time at university we had studied primates in general and the Great Apes in more detail. From this theoretical learning I knew a number of facts about our closest relatives which I found fascinating.

Firstly, in biological terms, the Great Apes were all part of the hominids family tree which includes orangutans, gorillas, bonobos, chimpanzees and humans. At the time it was appreciated that we were extremely closely related. However, we were to learn only just over a decade later exactly how close the relationships between the Great Apes actually were when scientists researched and compared the genomes of this family. When they studied the percentages of DNA which humans shared with the other Great Apes their astounding results were as follows:

Chimpanzees 99%
Bonobos 98.6%
Gorillas 98%
Orangutans 97%

Secondly, that like humans, the gorillas, bonobos and chimpanzees were social beings who chose to live in vibrant and highly interactive communities all of which had specific and intricately developed cultural behaviours. Some displayed grouped hunting tactics and strategies based upon cooperation and coordination of effort. Within their societies they showed consciousness of rank and status which influenced their interactions and position in the group. On the other hand, the orangutans were very different in this aspect of their behaviour, living rather semi-solitary lives within their rainforest environments. Typically orangutan populations would be loosely scattered across their home territory, with one male servicing perhaps a small group of three to five individual females who would also live separately raising their infants.

Thirdly, much like humans, the other Great Apes were all recognised as having intelligence levels which included the ability to learn to use symbols, sign language, understand aspects of human communication and memory of events over time. They could be manipulative and deceptive, as well as recognising themselves and members of their own family in photos. It was generally accepted that when compared with humans, they were as intelligent as a five or six year old child. [8]

Finally, it was also noted that, whilst humans and chimpanzees were acknowledged for their sometimes physically aggressive and tribe like behaviour, the orangutans did not display these traits. They were more passive and more likely to avoid confrontational events, appearing to lack the killer instinct regularly shown by ourselves and our closest cousins the chimpanzees. As you can imagine I was keen to interact with these enigmatic and fascinating beings as much as I could.

When that day finally came, I was shown how to clean their enclosures, given their diet sheets and instructed on how and when to feed them. From there, I was pretty much left to get on with it. Now, because of what I knew about the orangutans' behaviours, when I started working for them, I didn't worry too much that they could be potentially dangerous or that they could seriously injure me. And I certainly wasn't focussed upon the fact that they were physically stronger than me. Plus, I knew that Charlie used to go in with some of the orangutans during his time at the zoo. However as he got older and grew quite frail prior to his retirement, he had stopped entering the enclosures some time before he left. Thus, in my mind I had a clear slate so to speak and I thought, *"Oh well, I'll go in with them and see what happens,"* and that is just what I did.

Therefore I began to go in to the enclosures and sit with the orangutans whilst I had my lunch, which was definitely not usual practice in any other zoos to my knowledge. Mainly I chose to interact with the female orangutans such as Utama, Puteri, Punya and Puspa or with the younger adolescent males like Puluh. I felt no fear when I was with them, just a calm sense of awe and appreciation. It was an enormous privilege to spend this time with them at such close quarters. I would observe them and their particular behaviours as each orangutan had their own very distinct personalities and they were all highly intelligent, aware beings. Perhaps, most importantly, I really liked them as persons and felt an affinity and innate connection with them. What was even more rewarding was they appeared to like, and wish to connect with me too.

So for both myself and the orangutans it was a case of the more we got to know each other, the more we grew to like each other.

Hsing Hsing's Health Priority....

While settling into the Primate Section as the Head Orangutan Keeper and getting to know the orangutans as a group, I was met with my first major challenge to tackle. It was urgent and revolved around the health of one of the colony's adult, *cheek padder* males, Hsing Hsing, who had recently been diagnosed with diabetes.

The cause of Hsing Hsing's condition stemmed from the fact that he was not raised in Perth Zoo, instead he was born and raised at Singapore Zoo. More to the point, he was the son of that zoo's famous breakfast tea party orangutan named Ah Meng. Unfortunately it was customary for the Singapore Zoo to stage regular tea parties with Ah Meng and Hsing Hsing for the zoo visitors' entertainment. This meant that the orangutans involved were routinely fed sweets, lollies and sugary treats as well as been given drinks of coke and other soft drinks. Unfortunately this led to Hsing Hsing becoming diabetic, as orangutans are not able to cope with diets so high in refined sugar and so far removed from their natural eating habits. Therefore, when Hsing Hsing came to Perth he was already an unidentified diabetic. When he was diagnosed, I was given the task of working with Hsing Hsing using Positive Reinforcement Training (PRT) to get him to willingly allow his keepers to undertake his daily blood tests and give him his insulin injections. I had just six weeks to do it, and to add to this, Hsing Hsing had a reputation for being generally grumpy with humans due to his previous treatment at Singapore Zoo.

However I set to work with Hsing Hsing straight away and we began the PRT training together. This involved me demonstrating to him what was required, getting him to imitate the desired behaviour and then rewarding him with food treats for repeating the behaviours. In my mind I imagined that Hsing Hsing, a 100kg alpha male who was strong enough to rip my arms off, would not take kindly to the practice of having to present me with his out stretched hand. Let alone then allow me to give him a pin prick in his finger so we could take his blood to test. Once this was done he would then have to present his shoulder so we could inject him with insulin. This had to happen each day through the bars of his night enclosure.

Interestingly, after only a very short period of the training, I realised that Hsing Hsing was not actually responding to my commands or the PRT as such, but instead he was skilfully reading my body language. In this way, I learnt that orangutans mainly communicated with body language, so Hsing Hsing was naturally looking for body language cues, rather than verbal cues, when trying to determine what I wanted. Therefore he learnt everything needed within the six week timeframe. Additionally, this highly intelligent being not only learnt what to do, he seemed to understand that he needed his treatment and willingly co-operated with receiving it. I was both amazed and enthralled with how Hsing Hsing had dealt with this challenge and still to this day, he obediently puts out his hand to have his morning pin prick blood test and then offers his shoulder to his keeper to receive his insulin injection. (I must add here that the needles involved in Hsing Hsing's daily care had to be specially ordered in for the job because an orangutan's skin is as thick as leather on their hands. Which means that the only needle blades which are strong and big enough to pierce their skin are those made especially to cater for the thick skin of Yugoslav men.)

My formative contact with Hsing Hsing left a lasting and deep impression on me and over the coming years I was to enjoy many more humorous and inspiring encounters with this clever and compassionate orangutan.

Focussing Upon Mental Health and Wellbeing...

Over time, as I continued to work for them, I got to know the orangutans as individuals and started to learn more about the lives of their wild relatives in Sumatra and Borneo. I also began to recognise that even though Perth Zoo's orangutan population was relatively healthy and physically robust, I could see that we could be doing so much more for them in regards to their mental and psychological wellbeing. With the full support of my friend and mentor, Reg Gates, it was at this point that I began to introduce a program of Behavioural Enrichment (BE) for the orangutans as a way of offering them greater mental stimulation and challenge. We did this by enriching their daily lives with games, puzzles, play equipment, toys and food treats hidden within objects so they would have to use their keen intelligence to access the food. Not surprisingly, the orangutans loved this new approach and responded accordingly.

Prior to this additional activity, the primate keepers were only required to feed and clean the animals. So once we began the BE program, keepers necessarily had greater demands made upon their time and schedules. Because of this, we did meet with some resistance from both keepers and management. They felt that this was not only creating more work for everyone, but also they didn't always see the point in providing greater mental stimulation for the orangutans. They also complained that it made the enclosures 'look messy' and questioned why we should be concerned with offering them more meaningful activity and focussing upon their happiness. So I found that in some ways we had a fight on our hands to convince others of the importance of this work. However, it's also within my nature to want to improve and move things ahead and create positive change. I realised that some people embrace change, others resist it and some strongly object to it... but as a leader it's important to introduce change as a positive step forward, so I persisted, regardless.

Looking into the Eyes of the Orangutans...

As I mentioned earlier, Perth Zoo was recognised as a world leader for its orangutan breeding program. Furthermore, once we had Hsing Hsing's diabetes managed and under control, he was an active and excellent sire for the females. In late 1990, as part of this program, we had put an intelligent and gentle female named Puspa who was of breeding age in with Hsing Hsing and hoped that these two would successfully mate. Fortunately for us, Puspa soon fell pregnant and we all eagerly awaited the upcoming birth and the addition of her offspring to the colony.

Much like humans, female orangutans mature slowly and are able to breed at around 14 to 15 years of age and their gestation period is also around nine months. However, the main difference in their breeding cycle is that, once of age, the females only reproduce up to every nine years or so due to their long and devoted mothering of their young. Unfortunately this aspect of their reproductive habits makes them particularly susceptible to extinction. Therefore it was always great news when one of the zoo's females was expecting a baby.

After an uneventful and full term pregnancy, Puspa finally began to show signs that she was preparing herself for the imminent birth. As I was so deeply involved with the orangutans by this stage, and had a wonderful relationship with Puspa, of course I was present at the birth of her infant. This meant that I began staying in close proximity to the orangutan's night quarters and was on call for Puspa's impending shift to motherhood.

Within a few nights I was rewarded with the arrival of Puspa's first baby, a beautiful and lively little female named Sekara. I must say that it was definitely love at first sight when I laid eyes on the bright and curious Sekara. Because there is another interesting difference between orangutan and human babies, and this is that orangutan young are born aware and awake, able to see straight away and to interact with their mothers and the environment. In fact as soon as they are born you can immediately see their unique and vibrant little personalities within their eyes. With Sekara, as with all of the six or so other orangutan births at which I had the privilege of being present, I was always amazed at the responsiveness and awareness of the new born infants.

In addition to this, there was one other very special event which occurred after the birth of Sekara, which was to both fill my heart with awe and gratitude and also cement my deep love and connection with these beings.

To ensure that the mother and baby orangutans have the time and space to bond and begin to suckle, we made it common practice to keep them safe and secure within their night quarters for at least the first 48 hours after birth. So Puspa and Sekara were able to spend this precious time together. However after this time was over, and as soon as Puspa saw me come into the area behind her night quarters to check on her, she deliberately came over and sat next to the open mesh barrier separating us. And of course she was holding her precious newborn within her arms. Seeing her so close and sensing that she wanted me to interact with her, I sat down on the floor on the opposite side of the mesh barrier. I then watched in amazement as she carefully and slowly moved Sekara closer to the mesh, gently took her daughter's arm and proceeded to put Sekara's tiny little outstretched hand towards me. Instinctively I reached my fingers towards Sekara's open hand and she immediately grasped my finger within hers. In that instant as I looked into the eyes of both Puspa and her beautiful daughter Sekara, with her tiny yet perfectly formed fingers wrapped around mine, I saw the depth of love and trust which these truly unique beings possessed. I was moved beyond measure at the gesture of this devoted mother wishing to form a bond between her child and myself. It was a moment that I will never forget.

Within the next week or so, when I was able to again sit with Puspa and Sekara within their enclosure, this doting mother gently and deliberately placed Sekara into my arms for me to hold. Over the years I can say that after each orangutan birth I witnessed, the mothers would always have their infants hold my fingers within two days of their birth and shortly afterwards, would also give me their baby to hold. So I was given the opportunity to become part of this unique world which was something that not many other people have had the privilege of experiencing, because in the wild it just wouldn't happen.

It is events like these which I treasure for their beauty, truth and impact upon my life... At this point, I knew that I had found the work I loved and would continue to do on behalf of the orangutans for as long as I could. Furthermore, I realised that because of the experiences which I was having with the orangutans, I was also beginning to make big changes within myself. I was no longer able to see the orangutans, or any of the Great Apes, as being *other or different* from me and had come to the conclusion that they were not only sentient beings but *persons* in the true sense of the word.

From Hunter to Hippy- Taronga Park Zoo Exchange...

The changes I was experiencing within my working life also began to reflect upon my behaviours and attitudes in my personal life. Furthermore, the things which once attracted and excited me like fast cars, no longer seemed quite as important. I was also shifting in my approach to all living beings and had moved away from the *Hunter Type* of mentality which I first experienced when I joined the other keepers at the zoo.

Perhaps largely due to these shifts in perspective on my part, or perhaps not, but soon after Sekara's birth in 1991, I found myself in the middle of the breakdown of my first marriage. Feeling rather confused and at a loss, I decided to put my name forward for an inter zoo transfer and applied for a three month working exchange to Taronga Park Zoo, Sydney. I felt that the change of scenery would do me good and Taronga Park Zoo also offered the added opportunity to work with their large, 28 strong community of chimpanzees. Therefore in June 1992, I found myself settled into a make-shift bed in the hallway of a keeper share-house near the Sydney zoo and was looking forward to what the next three months would bring.

Being assigned to the African Animals Section which included the chimpanzees as well as a number of other animals, native to this region, I was enjoying the new environment and the fresh challenges it entailed. However about half way through my time there, a large female giraffe within my section had accidentally gone over a bollard when she was scared by some wind. In the incident the giraffe appeared to have been badly injured and unfortunately, after the vet's examination, we received the news that she had a severely broken front leg. Worse still, the fracture was not able to be repaired. Understandably for a giraffe this was a serious issue and ultimately the only possible course of action was to euthanize the animal.

As the giraffe was within my section, I was responsible for assisting during the whole procedure. This meant that I had to help corral the injured giraffe into her night quarters and then had to help hold down this huge living animal whilst the vet administered a lethal injection of poison, known as the '*green dream*'. So there I was, holding this frightened animal as it was slowly poisoned to death...

and I can tell you that the giraffe absolutely did not want to die. In fact it fought to live with every last ounce of its strength and will power.

As you can imagine it was a truly horrific and devastating event to be part of, especially as an animal lover and a zoo keeper who deeply cared for the animals with whom I worked. Furthermore, the animals I had euthanized in the past were always *killed* for the animals' sake because they were either suffering, in pain or at a point where they would not recover. However, the sudden and immediate horror I experienced at the killing of this giraffe made me understand not just intellectually, but also emotionally, that every living creature wants to live. In truth, they want this desperately as none of them wants to die. Therefore to take life away from another living being is shocking even when doing so for its own sake, out of compassion. Here I came to appreciate that, when it comes down to it, life is so precious and to kill for any reason other than on compassionate grounds is such a crime.

For me, this was a turning point and a culmination of the internal shifts which I had been going through. It was in this pivotal moment that I became a vegetarian, because I realised that no meat or taste of food was more important to me than the life of another living creature. I saw that no animal needed or deserved to die simply to satisfy my dietary desires, especially when I could operate perfectly well without meat in my diet. I no longer wanted the death of any animal on my hands nor, to have them killed out of sight on my behalf.

In addition to this key wake up moment regarding killing and eating meat, I also saw that I had an issue with the animals' suffering prior to their death. Because, no matter how humans try to rationalise and justify the suffering of livestock animals as humane, I had now experienced firsthand that the death of an animal was still a horrific incident. And this was so, even though we had tried to kill the giraffe as humanely as possible. The inescapable truth was that the giraffe didn't want to die. Therefore, for me, even if an abattoir could kill in a humane way, the slaughter of animals was no longer acceptable. In that moment I came to realise that there's no greater crime than to take away life from another living creature for no good reason... and I could not see any from this point forward.

I was almost 28 years old and I had made the shift from Hunter to Hippy.

From that moment onwards I began to make different choices about how I lived, how I ate and how I operated in the world. To begin with, I left meat eating behind and instead chose fresh plant based produce as well as free range eggs and some dairy products. Initially beginning with a vegetarian diet, I later moved to a vegan diet, which meant that I no longer ate any animal produce. This extended to not wearing leather or wool products and opting for canvas shoes and belts and woven cotton, hemp or linen jumpers and jackets. So my choices were based upon not having animals suffer for me, whether it was for my food or my clothing and in many ways it was a simple step to take. (I will be discussing my insights around this in Section 4 of the book)

SECTION 2

WHY ORANGUTANS?

"The world is beautiful to look at, but it is even more beautiful to understand."

Prof Brian Cox

CHAPTER 4
MEET THE ORANGUTANS

"Many people who look into an orangutan's eyes for the first time are profoundly affected by an obvious and intuitive discovery that 'humanity' extends beyond humanity"
Leif Cocks

My time at Taronga Park Zoo not only served to reinforce my new way of thinking and acting towards my fellow beings, as I became a practicing vegetarian. It also provided me with three months exposure to their large, intricately social chimpanzee community. Because at Perth Zoo I only had the opportunity to work with two chimpanzees, Jamie and Lollipop, who being only a solitary pair, had no opportunity to express the sociality and behaviour of normal chimpanzees. My focussed time with the expressive, demonstrative and somewhat aggressive chimps in Sydney, was in marked contrast to my interactions with the patient and thoughtful personalities of my orangutan friends back in Perth. Therefore after the zoo keeper exchange was over, I came home with a renewed appreciation for these unique beings and was even more aware of both the obvious and the more subtle differences orangutans exhibited from all other members of the Great Ape family.

So what makes the orangutans so distinctly different from the other members of the hominid family tree?

In my experience there are four specific areas which most characterise the orangutans:

1. Their Biology,
2. General Temperament,
3. Parenting and Early Years
4. Culture and Social Structure.

Importantly, to know and appreciate their unique traits goes a long way towards being able to understand, care for and respect these remarkable beings.

Orangutan Biology...

Found only on the islands of Borneo and Sumatra, orangutans have physically adapted to their rainforest jungle habitat and are the only Great Ape, except humans, to be found outside of Africa. The largest tree dwelling being in the world, generally orangutan males grow to around 1.5m in height with the smaller females reaching about 1.2m at maturity. Fully grown males can weigh anywhere between 93 to 130 kg, with females developing their body mass to around 48 to 55 kg. They are known to be exceptionally strong and use both their hands and feet for climbing trees, retrieving fruit and navigating through the jungle canopy with relative speed and grace.

Their hands are much like those of humans with four long fingers and an opposable thumb, however, their feet have four long toes with an opposable toe, making them more hand like. In fact, they are so adept in the use of their *feet as hands*, that they are often described as possessing *four hands*. In addition to this, the orangutans' arms stretch out longer than their bodies - over two metres from fingertip to fingertip - and these are skillfully used to employ a hook-grip which is perfect for their arboreal home environment, 6m to 30m above the forest floor. However, on the rare occasion that they travel on the ground, they walk on all fours, using their palms or their fists.

And although their life span in the wild is unknown, they are on record as living beyond 60 years within captivity, when provided with a reasonable captive environment.

Belonging to two quite distinct species, the Sumatran orangutan (*Pongo abelii*) and the Borneo orangutan (*Pongo pygmaeus*) they are genetically, behaviourally and physically different from each other. The physical differences being more obvious amongst the adult males of both species. This is because within each species, when male orangutans reach maturity and dominant status, they develop large cheek flanges and pendulous throat sacks which they use to make their characteristic male vocalization, the *long call*. The long call is used for a twofold effect, firstly to attract fertile females for possible mating and secondly to advertise their territorial presence to rival males in the vicinity.

More specifically, in the adult Sumatran males their cheek flanges form flat, fairly rigid, semi-circular discs at the sides of their face, of which Hsing Hsing is a perfect pin up boy handsomely demonstrating this aspect of the Sumatran species. Whereas, with the Bornean species, the male orangutans display heavier, less rigid cheek flanges. This results in them tending to protrude forward (especially when the male is overweight) and appearing more square in shape. Mature Sumatran orangutans also possess longer, lighter orange coloured and less lustrous hair than their Bornean cousins who are generally larger in size and have shinier, darker hair ranging from a deep red colour to a more chocolate brown hue. In addition to this, the beard of the adult male Sumatran orangutan is also longer, fuller, more pointed and lighter in colour.

Whilst the adult males and infants from each species are relatively easy to distinguish visually, it is more difficult to differentiate between the adult female orangutans and the sub adults or juveniles. This is because of the wide range of hair colour across the females and their lack of overt secondary sexual characteristics. In general, however, the adult female and juvenile Sumatran orangutans tend to display the lighter hair colouring and facial pigmentation of the males and in addition to this, they also possess beards, which grow more pronounced with age. In the case of the Bornean female orangutans, they have either very sparse beards or no beards at all and also display darker coloured hair. Overall, it is usually accepted that the Sumatran orangutans are the more fine featured and gracile of the two species, if not prettier, and I would have to agree with this summation.

Primarily fruit eaters, in their wild habitat, orangutans spend much of their day in the tree canopy foraging for food and feeding upon a wide range of vegetation. This includes, specific edible leaves, shoots, flowers, lianas, wood pith and bark. In addition to this they have been known to eat mineral soils, vines, fungi, orchids, termites, ants and other insects, leaf galls, cobwebs and bird's eggs. To gain an adequate water intake they suck and lick water from the surrounding vegetation and from their hair, when wet, as well as from naturally occurring water bowls in trees and from rivers if need be. [9]

General Temperament...

As I've already mentioned, from my experience with a range of captive as well as wild born orangutans, each of them has individual personality traits. However as semi-solitary, yet social beings, orangutans tend to have mild temperaments and embody what I can only say is a noble, selfless quality about them. In many ways this is because of the very fact that with a typical upbringing in the wild, they are reared to be independent and self-sufficient individuals. Therefore when they interact with humans at a deeper level they do not need or want anything from us and this is something which well adjusted, secure humans have in common with them.

Obviously, when orangutans are held in captivity, they necessarily are fully reliant upon us for all of their survival needs. But, even under these circumstances, for us to be able to share a relationship with a captive orangutan, demonstrates their innate capacity to connect with and wish to interact with us as other living beings. Furthermore, as someone who has had the privilege of getting to know and build relationships with orangutans over time, I have seen in their eyes a natural curiosity and inner light which seeks to connect with us. And in many ways, this connection can be a much truer one than those between humans, who are more chimpanzee like, in that we are beings who most often want something from each other. With orangutans, however, this contractual arrangement does not exist, as each being is independent and chooses to create the relationship on an equal footing.

Along with the peaceful and mild elements of their temperaments, orangutans also demonstrate a playful and even mischievous side to their being. In particular, when they are infants and still young pre-adolescents, orangutans are very childlike, extremely playful, engaging and fun-filled. They enjoy playing games, solving puzzles, climbing and observing the world around them from the relative safety of their mother's embrace. Juvenile orangutans can be found wrestling and play fighting with each other as well as engaging in exploratory play high up in the canopy whilst fearlessly navigating their tree environment far above the ground. Much like human beings, when juvenile orangutans reach adolescence around 12 to 15 years of age, males may associate in adolescent peer groups and the newly sexual males can even be particularly annoying to unsuspecting females… again in a way which is very similar to their human cousins.

This is not to say that orangutans do not get angry, jealous and aggressive and that I have not encountered badly behaved orangutans, because I have. In fact, I will say that Temara, the Perth Zoo born female orangutan, who ultimately we were able to release to the Sumatran wild in 2006, was definitely a fiery red head in every sense of the word. (I will share more of Temara's remarkable story in chapter 6) But usually there is a very good reason for the typically non-confrontational orangutan to exhibit aggressive behaviour. Such as, females who are nursing infants or protecting their young who may become defensive if they think that their offspring are being threatened; males competing for fertile females or territories; or orangutans who are under attack from predators seeking to defend or extricate themselves from a dangerous situation.

In fact, it has been recorded that, on occasion, humans have been attacked and injured by orangutans. This includes being bitten and even losing fingers, as orangutans defend themselves or attack to get food or objects which they want. However they won't attack to kill. This is in contrast to humans and chimpanzees who will attack and kill each other, slaughter the infants of other animals for food or as a demonstration of aggression. Because orangutans don't seem to have the internal intention or trigger to kill, even if they may want to hurt you or to get you away from their young or their females. To me it seems that they lack the killer instinct, which we humans unfortunately display all too often.

Interestingly, in the case of our interactions with our enigmatic orange cousins, it is known that across the centuries of human contact with these noble and peaceful creatures, we have been responsible for butchering at least 1,000,000 of them. However, the telling fact is that within all recorded history of our contact with them, whether in a zoo, the wild or in captivity in a sanctuary, there is no record of any orangutan ever killing a human being. The truth is that there was not one example of this. Yet humans have regularly hacked them to death with machetes, burnt them alive, shot their eyes out and riddled them with bullets. As well as killing mothers in front of their babies in order to steal their infants to be kept as caged pets or personal trophy animals.

Even when a mother orangutan is defending her baby she will

protect her offspring to her last breath in an attempt to save her young. She never kills the attacker even though she can be up to 7 times physically stronger than a human. Yet as a mother she steadfastly stands alone to protect her baby and will do everything within her power to avoid leaving her young at the mercy of humans. The equally remarkable fact is that adult male orangutans have canines as big and as strong as a tiger, and at the same time they are recognised as being up to 10 times as powerful as any human being. They have been known to defend themselves and potentially injure an attacker to escape, however they have not killed a human even though they are physically capable to do so.

Furthermore it is considered that the low, deep reverberating *long call* which adult male orangutans send out into the forest is also used as a pre-warning signal for other males in the area. Ensuring that they can move out of each other's paths as they travel through the forest. In this way they do not have to confront each other, un-necessarily. And even when males do clash, they charge at each other and break branches in shows of strength and dominance in order to scare one of the duelers away. If they do come to blows, they will grapple and bite each other, but rarely if ever, with the intention of killing their opponent. If death does occur, it is usually as a result of the injuries they have sustained in the fight which later become infected and fester within their tropical forest environment, rather than the fight itself. Such is the temperament and general demeanor of orangutans, perhaps we as humans could learn much from these beings?

Parenting and Early Years...

It is no coincidence that in the award winning book "*The Life of Pi*" and the major motion picture of the same name, that Pi's mother was represented by a female orangutan named Orange Juice.

[10] This is because orangutan mothers are recognised across the animal kingdom as being the archetypical maternal figures. Without a doubt, they are the most devoted, loving and nurturing mothers of all, even out performing human mothers in their care of their young.

As mentioned earlier, when describing the story of the birth of Puspa's baby, Sekara, female orangutans mature and are ready to reproduce at around the age of 14 to 15 years of age. Once pregnant, their gestation lasts around 8.5 to 9 months and they generally give birth at night in the relative safety of their night nest within the tree canopy. As orangutan males are involved only in the reproductive process as sires, orangutan mothers are solely responsible for the rearing of their young. Mothers usually give birth to a single infant and very rarely give birth to twins. This is due to the fact that the level of dedicated care and nurturing which they shower upon their young, a single infant is the most manageable for the mother. Infants are breast fed for up to six years of age and for the first four to six years of their life, the young orangutans cling to their mother's body as she navigates through the forest in search of fruit and other vegetation.

Even once the young are weaned from their mother's milk, they will still cohabit with her for a number of years. This is because she continues to pass on to them all of the knowledge they need to know in order to live an independent and semi-solitary life as an adult. Such is the depth and breadth of the female orangutan's mothering style that females in the wild only reproduce on average every eight to nine years, depending on the species and/or sub-species, to allow for the young to mature sufficiently before she mates again.

This demonstrates that under natural circumstances baby orangutans have the most loving, nurturing, caring and affectionate upbringing of any animal. And although a baby orangutan can cry, it is almost unheard of to ever hear a baby orangutan cry in the wild, because it just doesn't happen. This is due to the mothers' dedication to their babies as the young are constantly on their mother's body receiving love, attention and affection. In short, a female orangutan mother is devoted to her baby and her task of raising her child and whilst she is doing so she literally gives her whole life to her infant. The result of this is that naturally raised orangutans are very independent and confident as young and adolescents.

Seeing this type of nurturing first hand from orangutan mothers explains many aspects of these secure and peaceful beings' nature. Furthermore, it also puts paid to the idea of bringing up human children using *tough love* principles to engender strength and independence within the child. Obviously the reverse is true, as children reared this way become insecure, disconnected and brutalised in many ways. It is important to note what the internationally recognised primate expert, Jane Goodall, said of the chimpanzees at Goon River. It was here that she studied the chimpanzees in their wild communities and found that it was the male chimpanzees with the most loving, affectionate and caring mothers who rose through the ranks to become the dominant males. In addition to this, it was these males who ultimately became the leaders of their groups.

Therefore it would follow that if young intelligent beings are raised and loved, nurtured and given a caring secure environment, they will become confident, secure, independent and potentially dominant in life. This is clearly demonstrated by the depth of inner security and compassion evident within naturally raised orangutans. The intensity of care during their upbringing is because orangutans have to live in a mostly solitary situation in the rainforest and make all of their decisions for themselves. Therefore it is imperative that they be completely independent and competent to survive as they don't have the group, community or tribe to rely upon.

I was lucky enough to witness and then experience for myself the importance of the mothering bond between a mother orangutan and her young offspring during my early years as the Head Orangutan Keeper at Perth Zoo.

Raising Sekara....

I introduced you to the beautiful little baby female orangutan, Sekara, and her devoted mother Puspa in my earlier story of her zoo birth, in Chapter 3.

For the first two years all went very well for this mother and daughter duo, however when Sekara was around two years old she caught her toe in a climbing rope within their enclosure and unfortunately it was damaged quite badly. As soon as I cut Sekara free of the rope, we had the vet clean, treat and bandage the wound, and place Sekara back into the enclosure with her mother. However, the problem was that Puspa refused to leave the bandaged toe alone to heal and insisted on continually picking at the wound. To the extent that unfortunately over time it became severely infected and we had no other option but to amputate Sekara's toe.

Subsequently, once the operation was performed, we were very reluctant to put Sekara back into the enclosure with her mother for fear that a similar thing would occur with the newly completed surgery and stitches. Therefore we put Sekara's foot and leg in plaster to protect them from explorative little hands and we decided that I would take over the role of raising Sekara for the short time that it would take for the surgery to heal.

Understandably it was very important for Puspa to maintain as much visual and actual contact with her beloved baby as possible, so I set up camp opposite the orangutans' night quarters area whilst I hand raised Sekara. We would sleep within sight of Puspa, so she could see that Sekara was still close by and to prevent her from fretting for her child. During the days before opening hours at the zoo, I would take Sekara out on my rounds about the zoo grounds and she would hang on to me with her arms wrapped around my neck and chest as we wandered through the different sections. Sekara loved seeing all of the other animals and enjoyed the experience of viewing the bigger environment beyond the orangutan section and her enclosure.

I will never forget on one occasion when I took Sekara into the food store area where all of the Primate Section's fresh fruit and provisions were stored...as there was an absolute abundance of fresh fruit of all varieties literally packed from floor to ceiling. I looked down at Sekara and saw her total wonder and awe at the unexpected sight of all of this food. It was like we had just discovered a treasure trove. Immediately her little face and eyes lit up with excitement when she saw crates and crates of fruit, and suddenly she was trying to grab as much of the fruit as was possible to hold in her four little hands...

It was an unforgettable sight and I must say that raising Sekara for that six week period was one of the most enjoyable and personally rewarding times of my zoo career. The weeks that we shared together meant that Sekara and I were always particularly close due to the bonding we experienced. Needless to say that her devoted mother Puspa was much relieved and happy when I finally presented her daughter, with the newly healed toe, back into her care.

Dad Time with Atjeh...

Having said this about orangutan mothers, I have witnessed a great degree of patience and tolerance from a captive alpha male named Atjeh, towards his cheeky and playful offspring, Puluh. In this instance we had Atjeh's young son Puluh in his enclosure with him while his mother Puan was in courtship. Atjeh was a large and handsome male with the typical long orange dreadlocked body hair hanging from his arms and legs. We had seen Puluh playing with Atjeh on their climbing frame and had noticed that Puluh had taken a particular liking to the practice of swinging, dangling and hanging from Atjeh's long hair. We had also observed Atjeh tolerating this uncomfortable play session with great patience.

Before the next session of play with Atjeh and his offspring, however, we were very amused to see Atjeh sitting high up on this climbing frame and carefully tucking away all of his long arm strands of hair under his feet in preparation for the arrival of the cheeky Puluh. This is only what can be described as fatherly love and patience and was a unique situation to observe, as this would be highly unlikely to occur in nature.

Culture and Social Structure...

As already stated, orangutans are semi-solitary, yet social beings and have their own very distinctive and rich social system. Although in the wild, contact and interaction is less physical than that seen amongst the other Great Ape species, it is none the less a key element of their psychological wellbeing. Having a relatively dispersed social system, the orangutans create both space and a level of connection between neighbouring individuals and this social structure contributes to their welfare and continued health in natural environments. How this occurs is via the distinctly different behaviour of the males of the species and the females.

As the sex which *disperses* within the species, adult and adolescent males will leave the territory of their childhood to explore and discover new feeding areas and new female orangutans with whom to breed. Because of this they are known to roam across many square kilometres of forest range and they can be both resident and nomadic. Dominant adult males will set up a resident territory which may include the home territories of up to five adult females, as long as there is not an existing male in residence. So the male is positioned high up in the canopy within a central radius of the local breeding females. If there is already an alpha male present, they may engage in territorial behaviour until one male gains dominance and remains in the area, with the other moving on to find new territory. A dominant male may also leave an area where all of the resident breeding females have offspring, as we know that it can be up to nine years before they are once again ready to breed.

On the other hand, the females of the species tend to spend their whole lives in one patch of forest or one single territory. As the young female orangutans mature they tend to stay in the adjacent or neighbouring areas of their mothers once they move on from their care, which means that most females within one area are related to each other. Therefore female orangutans tend to stay put within their home range and rear their young within familiar surroundings where they nest high up in the tree canopy. Socially they are aware of each other and can often even see each other in the neighbouring trees, yet they afford each other the space with which to feed, nest and rear their young.

Translating Orangutan Social Behaviour in Captive Life.....

However, with orangutans in captivity a little knowledge can be a dangerous thing, because zoos and those keeping orangutans captive, consider them to be either *solitary* or *social* animals, yet fail to realise the deeper picture of their natural social systems. Therefore, unfortunately what I have seen occur is that orangutans are routinely kept in small groups, or they are kept alone and isolated. On the other hand, thinking that they are social animals, inexperienced keepers, collect a group of randomly clustered orangutans and put them all together into one small enclosure, expecting them to be happy. The problem within both scenarios is that, much like humans, orangutans are often psychologically and physically stressed under these conditions.

I think the best way to describe the situation for captive

orangutans is to use an analogy from our own human experience.

Imagine that they are like us. You and I may choose to share our home with other people, but certainly not with just anyone. For example, partners, close family or friends would be welcome in our home as long as they fitted comfortably into the established domestic arrangements in place. However, it would be quite unacceptable for a stranger to move into our personal space. Unsurprisingly, orangutans are exactly the same, in that they elect to live alone within dispersed family units as this is their natural preference. Just like us, they respect their family unit and choose to not share their home territories with just anyone. In this we both have a choice.

This is clearly demonstrated with humans who choose to live in the countryside and rural areas where people are spread out far and wide across large distances. In these areas there are often no fences and when individuals do meet up, everyone is very friendly and welcoming. Because they infrequently cross paths in daily life, when they do interact they get on well. Additionally, they can communicate via the phone like the orangutans do with their long calls across large distances in the forest.

However, when people move to the suburbs within closer proximity, you can see that fences tend to go up between each residence as they are now living at close quarters. Usually, people are a little less friendly, and maintain some degree of privacy and personal space. Then, when individuals or families move into a modern inner city environment, living in apartments or units at even closer proximity, you can see that people put walls up. In fact, often they don't speak to, or interact with one another, even though they may walk past each other every day. Strangely enough, this is often a natural response to inner city living for humans because it is how we cope with the situation.

Therefore when you take an orangutan- who is naturally like a person from the countryside - and put them into a situation akin to inner city living, for example, a zoo, it is easy to comprehend what each individual has to do to survive. It is no wonder that they have to put up those walls in order to cope with the social restrictions occurring within these circumstances. Hence zoos operating without insight into how orangutans function in the wild, will often put all of these unique beings into one enclosure together. As you can imagine, the result is that the orangutans experience ongoing mental stress within these situations. Or, alternatively, they put them into an enclosure alone, much like solitary confinement, and again mental stress occurs for the captive being.

However, over time, what we were able to do at Perth Zoo, was to house our orangutans within an enclosure environment which mimicked and maintained their natural social structure. We were the only zoo in the world to do this. Interestingly we couldn't use trees and wood for these enclosure structures as the orangutans destroy these in superfast time. So the answer lay in utilising movable metal structures which resulted in enclosures which may not have looked particularly natural, but which were actually far more suited to the orangutans' wellbeing than the accepted "natural looking" zoo enclosures. In this way we were able to put the interests of the orangutans first, rather than those perceived by the zoo's management. As always I think that love and respect finds a way...and although it took many years, we were ultimately able to totally redesign their climbing structures and enclosures to more closely reflect their living situation in the wild. This included working with orangutans' ergonomics and consulting with an architect to design and build structures which moved with the orangutans and provided them with an artificial canopy and nesting structures which mimicked their vertical behaviour in the forest.

In addition to this, all of the adult females were located within their own "territories" or enclosures next to their mothers. By doing so all of the related females could see each other and interact with each other from the top of their own high level climbing frames.

The alpha males were obviously housed separately within their own enclosures, unless they were breeding with an adult female. Because each individual could see the others over long periods of time, they were able to maintain both their mental health and happiness. The only barrier to their total happiness was of course that they didn't have ultimate control over their environment as they would have in the wild, but at least we could create a home which came as close to this as possible. However, I was beginning to appreciate that the only way we could guarantee happiness for the orangutans was to have them live free and wild in their natural habitat.

Working with Reg at the Zoo...

Meanwhile on the human front at the zoo, I was also learning about leadership and working within teams. As we all know, a work place is greatly impacted by its management team, both the great and the not so great. Unfortunately during this time at the zoo, the latter was the case which meant that Reg was often at odds with the zoo's management. This only worsened as Reg continued to fight for the welfare of his much loved primates, including proposals for improved conditions and better facilities. It was because he was so heartfelt and passionate about the wellbeing of the animals in his care, that he just couldn't understand why the people at the top were blocking his decisions to improve things for them. Over time he began to feel impotent to change things under these trying circumstances, and it started to tear him apart on a personal level.

In addition to this, I suppose it certainly didn't help his cause that he was friendly with me, who by this time had been elected –in my absence- by the staff as the zoo's rather outspoken Shop-Steward for the Miscellaneous Workers Union. As I was known to be slightly unconventional and more likely to be found in a tie-dyed t-shirt than my zoo uniform, I'm sure that this added to his alienation from management.

For example, on one occasion, in my position as the union representative, I had approached the then current zoo director about a rumour I had heard regarding a directive from the zoo's board. Apparently, the directive came straight from the Board President and required that the orangutan babies be taken away from their mothers so they could be displayed at shopping centres to promote the zoo. Of course the response I was expecting from the director was, *"Don't worry we won't let that happen."* But to my dismay, the response I received was, *"You will do exactly what you are told or you can leave the zoo."* I was stunned. However, not to be deterred and as a lateral thinker, I came up with a third option for the director. So after a lengthy industrial action by the staff, the zoo's director was moved sideways and eventually removed from the zoo.

Of course, there were other animal welfare and staff issues which justified the director's removal and Reg was usually caught in the middle of most of them. Because of this he would often ask me to attend any tense or potentially confrontational meetings with him, for moral support. In fact, I remember a time when we were chatting in the orangutan keeper raceway and discussing an upcoming meeting which Reg had asked me to attend. I recall saying to him that, *"We need to be strong to see this situation through otherwise I am concerned about what would happen to the animals."* I was deeply saddened when an anguished and broken set of eyes met mine and Reg said, *"That's just it Leif, I am not sure that I am strong enough anymore."*

It was a sad thing to see how poor management could negatively impact good people… people of worth and commitment. But it was even worse to see Reg become alienated and destroyed in the process. Unfortunately Reg began to drink as a coping mechanism…

CHAPTER 5
SMARTER THAN YOU THINK

"Fu Manchu was an orangutan who crafted a key from wire to escape from his exhibit at Omaha Zoo. His keepers had trouble figuring out how he did it, as he would hide the key in his mouth whilst they were around."
Curious Wanderer

By the mid 1990's I felt as if I had begun to hit my stride with my work and my life.

Firstly, in 1993, I met a beautiful, strong minded young woman, named Wendy and shortly after this we began dating. I remember the first time I laid eyes on her, one Sunday afternoon, at Perth Zoo where she was acting as a Zoo Guide. I had been doing my usual rounds and had come across Wendy as she was viewing the Sulawesi Crested Macaques enclosure. Immediately intrigued by the sight of this gorgeous curly-haired redhead, I strode off to find my friend, the head of the Zoo Guides, to introduce us. Unfortunately, by the time we returned to the exhibit, she had gone.

However coincidentally, the next weekend whilst I was looking after the tamarins, Wendy had been asked to manage visitors in the Walk-Through Tamarin Exhibit, so I was in luck. Not wanting to miss this opportunity, I started a conversation with her. Happily, I had the distinct impression that Wendy liked me too, because she started to play with my Indian hair braids under the yellow bandanna I was wearing at the time. Wanting to make sure that I caught up with her again soon, I arranged to meet her at an upcoming zoo function. After a short separation, whilst I was in Sumatra visiting an orangutan release site, we started seeing each other on a regular basis.

Secondly, I had learned so much from my formative years as a keeper at the Perth Zoo and more still during the equally intensive early years as the Head Orangutan Keeper in the Primate Section. I realised I had gained much in the way of practical experience through my contact with the zoo's orangutans and had branched out to volunteer with their wild relatives in Sumatra and Borneo. During this time I had also come to the conclusion that I loved my work for orangutans, knew I had found a purpose through my career and a cause to which I could commit. However, I also understood there was so much more to be done on behalf of the captive and free populations of orangutans around the world. With this in mind, I decided to go back to university with the aim of combining my hands-on zoo experience with a deeper, research based study of my favourite subject…orangutans and their behaviour.

So between the years of 1994 to 1998, I completed a Post Graduate Diploma on, *the effects of zoo visitors on cage utilization of primates*, followed by a Master of Science focussing upon *the key factors affecting the health and well-being of captive orangutans*. Now, I can understand, to some minds, these areas of study may have seemed rather dry and uninteresting. However I was determined to find a way to help improve conditions for captive orangutans. Furthermore, I was curious to learn all I could in order to do so. In my daily work I had come to know and love the resident orangutans with whom I had shared so many important life moments, and had formed deep and lasting friendships with many of them. As a zoologist and keeper I had learned so much about the Sumatran and Bornean orangutans as separate species and I had begun to see that perhaps the number one defining feature of orangutans, *their keen intelligence*, was also the cause of their suffering in captivity. At this point, I began to question how I could reconcile this situation within myself.

Orangutans, Smarter Than the Average Ape...

In the Malay and Indonesian languages, *orang* means "person" and *utan* is derived from *hutan*, which means "forest." Therefore, within the languages of Indonesia and Malaysia, *orangutan* literally means "person of the forest." The recognition of orangutans as being persons is not only reflected within their name, it is also accepted that many of the Dayak tribes from the regions also considered the orangutans to be *persons* belonging to another tribe. Some of these tribes actively hunted and killed the orangutans as a food source, whilst others had strict prohibitions, on moral grounds, against killing or injuring them. However, no matter what the local approach was to their orange, tree dwelling neighbours, the indigenous peoples also acknowledged the orangutans for their innate intelligence. So, in their natural environment, orangutans have a history of being recognised both for their personhood and their remarkable mental acuity.

On the other hand, as someone who has worked for a number of years with a variety of Great Apes from all over the world, in captivity and in the wild, I have found that many in the conservation field believe that the most intelligent Great Apes, after humans, were the chimpanzees, bonobo and then the gorillas. This was probably because these apes are known to be closer to humans, both genetically and behaviourally. However, I have not yet come across an experienced primate keeper who has worked closely with all the Great Ape species who does not believe that orangutans are by far the most intelligent of these. This is definitely something I have come to know as true after witnessing countless instances of their undoubted ingenuity and resourcefulness.

This is not to say that the other Great Apes are *not intelligent*, but that orangutans are just that bit smarter on many levels. Perhaps it is the combination of their temperament and the way they apply their minds to situations, because to me there is a significant difference

between the intelligence of orangutans and other Great Apes. I think
that the following two aphorisms - often shared amongst Great Ape
keepers - clearly illustrate this fact.

1. *"Give a screwdriver to a chimpanzee and it will throw it at
   another chimpanzee...*
   *Give a screwdriver to a gorilla and it will use it to
   scratch itself...*
   *Give a screwdriver to an orangutan and it will use it
   to escape!"*
2. *"Give ten problems to a chimp and it will solve six of the
   problems in 30 mins and never solve the remaining four.*
   *Give ten problems to an orangutan and it will take one week,
   but will solve all ten of the problems."*

So given we know that, excepting humans, all Great Apes are
as intelligent as a five to six year old child, what is it which makes
orangutans' intelligence so noteworthy?

From experience I have identified the following key areas of
intelligence in orangutans:

- Thinks and then acts, with strong reasoning and problem
  solving capability
- Exhibits self-awareness
- Demonstrates *Theory of Mind*
- Comprehension of language and communication signs
- Excellent spatial memory and recognition of events and
  people over time

Thinks and Then Acts...

As the aphorisms above suggest, orangutans have keen problem solving and reasoning skills which they use to great effect over time. I think that's why orangutans are often characterised as being thoughtful and considered apes, because on many occasions they are mentally observing situations, turning these over in their minds and literally figuring things out for themselves. For them the practice of thinking first before acting provides them with an innate ability to *respond* to a situation, rather than impulsively *react* to it. This enables orangutans to be governed by a greater depth of learned wisdom instead of being driven by instinct and reactions alone. And I must say that this is stark contrast to the highly emotional, demonstrative and immediately reactive behaviour of the chimpanzees with whom I worked at Perth and Taronga Park Zoos.

However, I have witnessed this ability to think, reason and then act with countless numbers of our orange cousins and none more clearly than when a captive orangutan figures out how to escape from their enclosures....and yes, orangutan escapes do happen at zoos. In fact I will go as far to say that, without exception, anyone who has cared for a captive orangutan will have experienced at least one instance of a planned or opportunistic escape attempt from these ingenious beings, and if they say that they haven't, I would suggest they haven't worked with them quite long enough yet!

A Ladder to Freedom...

I recall the first time I saw a well-considered orangutan escape plan in action was very early on in my zoo keeping career with the primates. I had observed one of the female adult orangutans, Mawas (which is an indigenous name for orangutans), who seemed to be unusually interested in an old face brick wall on one side of her enclosure. However, whenever I approached her enclosure she would move away from the brick wall and appear to be interested in something else. On closer inspection I discovered that she had been meticulously removing the loose mortar around every third brick in a line up the wall. What this meant was that she could remove the evenly spaced bricks to form a ladder which she could use to climb up the side of the wall and out to freedom or perhaps a quick visit with a neighbouring male? She would disguise her clever escape plan by putting the bricks back into the wall every time she heard me coming her way.

Because I was so new to working for the orangutans I was both surprised and impressed at the level of forethought, planning and deception which Mawas exhibited with executing her escape. I was officially put on notice to be aware of just how ingenious orangutans could be. And it wasn't too long before I encountered another more opportunistic orangutan escape in action, but this time it was a mother and son team.

A Ladder of a Different Kind...

On this occasion, I had been doing some work in the orangutan night quarters and was walking along a raceway between them. At the same time my mentor and friend Reg Gates was visiting the section and had popped in to say, "*Hi.*" So as we were chatting I could see what was going on in the off-limit areas behind him. As we were in the middle of our conversation something caught my eye over Reg's shoulder. I momentarily shifted my gaze towards the movement and saw one of the young male orangutans, Puluh, walking casually past the window facing me. In that split second, it didn't actually register what I had just seen and I continued my conversation with Reg.

However, only seconds later I saw his mother, Puan, walk by the same window and stop to peer in as she, just as casually, wandered by.

Suddenly I stopped mid-sentence and said to Reg quite matter-of-factly, "*The orangutans have escaped.*" Reg looked at me and asked, "*What do you mean the orangutans have escaped?*" A strange question for an equally strange statement, I know, but in that moment Reg couldn't believe or comprehend what I'd just said. And I'll admit that, at the time, it must have appeared like we were involved in some kind of zoo based comedy sketch. Anyway, we immediately jumped into action and headed out to find where these two had gone. Rushing up to the roof overlooking the enclosures we could clearly see how they had escaped and where they had headed.

Firstly, a large banana tree had over turned outside their enclosure and part of it had fallen into Puan and six year old Puluh's exhibit. Being orangutans it was a relatively simple task for them to see that the solid trunk and banana leaves could easily be used to form the perfect green bridge to climb up and over the wall of their enclosure. Taking this irresistible opportunity, Puluh, the young male, had expertly clambered along the banana tree and had climbed up and out of the enclosure. Seeing her son in the process of leaving, Puan, his protective and curious mother, had quickly followed suit. After having a bit of a look around to weigh up their options it appears that they chose to go in different directions.

Puluh had chosen to jump in to an adjacent enclosure with Mawas, the 56 year old Bornean female orangutan of whom I spoke earlier in this chapter. Because of this choice he was able to have his first sexual experience with an unrelated female and mate with her, even being able to remain there for a short interlude with his *older woman*. (It is an interesting fact that if you give a male orangutan a choice between an older female and a younger one, the males always choose the older one as they are seen to be more experienced and possessing superior mothering skills.) Meanwhile, once Puan had seen that Puluh was occupied in the enclosure with Mawas, and not to be outdone by her son, she chose to jump into the enclosure occupied by Hsing Hsing, the adult male. Puan also managed to have a brief affair with Hsing Hsing before later being moved back to her enclosure. Therefore our opportunistic escape was averted, simply by the choice of the orangutans.

Self-Awareness...

Orangutans clearly possess self-awareness and a distinct sense of themselves and others as separate entities. I have not only observed orangutans demonstrating self-awareness first hand, but it has also been scientifically proven that amongst the Great Apes, all are able to exhibit this trait repeatedly.

The concept of self-awareness in orangutans was first raised as a possibility as far back as 1838. As the story goes, the renowned biologist and evolutionary theorist, Sir Charles Darwin was observing the behaviour of a captive orangutan named Jenny whilst visiting the London Zoo. Apparently he witnessed Jenny become agitated and extremely upset, much like a young child, after being teased with an apple by her keeper. After viewing this event Darwin began to consider the subjective experience of an orangutan and thought about how Jenny might view what had just occurred. During the same visit Darwin was able to watch Jenny look into a mirror and gaze at her own reflected image and he later noted his impression that she had recognised herself in the reflection. [11]

Inspired by this idea of Darwin's, in the 1970's psychologist, Gordon Gallup, devised a behavioural assessment technique called the Mirror Test or the Mark Test to determine whether non humans, in this case, Great Apes were able to demonstrate self-recognition. Basically the test subjects were first put into an empty room with a large mirror to gauge their responses. When self-recognition was present, the test subjects went through four stages of behaviour and cognition, including:

1. Social responses
2. Physical inspection (e.g. looking behind the mirror)
3. Repetitive mirror-testing behavior
4. Realization of seeing themselves

The orangutan and chimp subjects were able to recognise themselves in the mirror, whilst at least in this trial, the bonobos and gorillas were not. Following this, the test subjects were then anesthetised and subsequently marked on their faces with a red dye and placed back into the room with the mirror. Once awake, the orangutans clearly demonstrated that when they saw the red mark on their face in their reflected image, they recognised that they were seeing the mark upon themselves. They therefore proceeded to touch the mark on their face to discover what it was and attempted to remove it. [12]

It is also well documented that Chantek, the famous signing orangutan, displayed self-awareness when grooming himself in a mirror and also by his understanding and use of role playing, in that he could play games like Simon Says and role reversals. Remember that Chantek also exhibited comprehension of me as another being with whom he could communicate when we first met in the primate centre, so he was aware of himself and myself as two separate beings. To me the self-awareness of orangutans is incontrovertible. Furthermore, after so many years of working for orangutans and clearly experiencing their high levels of self-awareness, I find it difficult to understand that some humans still question the idea that they possess this ability.

Theory of Mind...

As a progression from the concept of orangutans' self-awareness and intelligence is their demonstration of Theory of Mind (ToM).

Basically the Theory of Mind is:

"..the ability to attribute mental states—beliefs, intents, desires, pretending, knowledge, etc.—to oneself and others and to understand that others have beliefs, desires, intentions, and perspectives that are different from one's own." [13]

This means a being is able to discern that they have their own thoughts and desires, as well as appreciating that others also have different thoughts and desires of their own. It also follows that a being demonstrating Theory of Mind would be able to recognise the difference between acts performed intentionally from those occurring accidentally. And it has been proven that orangutans and chimps can make the distinction between accidental and intentional acts. This being the case in the scientific world, I also have years of practical proof of Theory of Mind amongst my orangutan friends.

The Early Adventures of Mawas ...

After my early encounter with Mawas and her ladder building escape attempt, I was not surprised when older staff informed me that this wasn't the first time she tried this and that the wily and determined Mawas had devised another ingenious escape plan. However, in this one she had succeeded.

The incident occurred before I started on the Primate Section and apparently Mawas had somehow convinced an orangutan in the enclosure next to hers, to throw his plastic fruit crate over the wall and into her enclosure. Now for obvious reasons, the primate keepers had strict rules to ensure that each orangutan only had access to one standard plastic fruit crate per enclosure, to prevent escapes. So when Mawas had the two crates at her disposal, she went straight into her enclosure's moat and stacked her new crate on top of her own crate at the base of the moat. She then arranged for her enclosure mate, a younger female orangutan named Utama, to stand on top of both crates. Mawas then expertly climbed on top of Utama's shoulders, grabbed the over-hanging bougainvillea plant and clambered out of her enclosure.

However at that same moment one of the zoo keepers saw Mawas hanging from the top of the moat, just over the public guard rail. Reacting quickly, he decided to hit Mawas's hands in order to encourage her to fall back into her enclosure. However this short term thinking by the keeper did not have any effect on Mawas, except that she was deeply offended by the act of violence on her person. So once she was free and out in the public area she approached the offending zoo keeper, sat on him and bit into his calf with her large teeth. The keeper recalled to me the horror of feeling Mawas's teeth meet inside his calf muscle. Once Mawas had seen that justice had been served, she wandered around the zoo grounds with the public for some time, until finally she was man-handled by ten zoo keepers into a cage and returned to her enclosure, minus the second crate.

Mawas Strikes Again...

This was not the only time that Mawas had vented her anger on a keeper for not being able to do as she pleased. Previously, before the current open enclosure exhibit was built at the zoo, the orangutans were held in old primate cages which had very dark, small night quarters to the rear. However, the problem was that Mawas was claustrophobic and would not enter the confined and dark night quarters whilst they were being cleaned. So during the regular cleaning, she was allowed to wander around the keepers' raceway at the back until cleaning was completed. This was standard practice at the time because of her phobia and as Mawas was a trusted zoo inmate.

However, one day during cleaning time she decided to go over and interact with a baby orangutan housed at the end of the area. Not wanting Mawas to let the young orangutan out of its night quarters, John, the keeper, yelled at her to, *"Stop!"* Afterwards he recalled the indignant look Mawas gave him for his gall at yelling at her and knew right way that he was in trouble. Sure enough, Mawas threw him across the raceway before returning to her cleaned enclosure in what could only be termed as a *huff*.

Hsing Hsing's Escape…

It is well documented that orangutans will carefully watch their keepers lock and unlock doors when securing them, and are therefore well aware of the routine procedure and the process which in entails. So if a keeper happens to miss any element of the security process, the orangutans will be well aware of the fact, even if the keeper isn't. On one occasion, this specific situation occurred during the mid-day movement where a keeper somehow forgot to properly lock down and secure the door on Hsing Hsing's night quarters.

Obviously wise to this fact, Hsing Hsing apparently waited for the keeper to leave the area and when the coast was clear he carefully and quietly let himself out into the keepers' area behind all of the other orangutan night quarters. Now, instead of making a run for it himself, Hsing Hsing then spent his time in an attempt to open all of the locks on the night quarters of his fellow orangutans in order to set them free. And that is where he was discovered when a keeper came into to check on things. As you can appreciate, Hsing Hsing's actions

Perth's rescue,
Kalimantan

Chantek at
Primate Centre,
USA

Dinar at Perth Zoo

Mum, Angel and I, Sydney 1966

Mum, Angel and I, Hong Kong 1972

Dad, Angel and I, Hong Kong 1972

First Dog 'Kelly' at Home in Perth, WA

Charlie Broomfield with Atjeh in early concrete enclosure, Perth Zoo

Rosemary Markham and orangutan, Perth Zoo
(credit Rosemary Markham)

Reg Gates, Puteri and I share a laugh, Perth Zoo

With an orangutan during contact session, Perth Zoo

Hsing Hsing

A cuddle with Puteri

Sekara with her injured toe

Puluh, the cheeky son of Atjeh

Mawas with her crate

Puan

The Orangutan Project- original board, 1998

Wendy and I get married, Vegas 1999

Puteri with baby Temara

Kylie Bullo, Punya and I

Celebrating a 1st birthday
with Kylie

New enclosures Perth Zoo

New enclosures Perth Zoo

Painting with Puteri and Jane
Goodall, Perth Zoo (taken through
enclosure glass)

Tatok playing under a large
leaf at jungle school

Peter Pratje and I, in the rainforest

Meeting Temara again, wild and free
(credit Peter Pratje)

Goodbye my friend Puteri

Leuser after being blinded (credit Sumatran
Orangutan Conservation Project)

Gober with her twins, Ginting and Ganteng (credit Sumatran Orangutan Conservation Project)

Gober and Ginting, free in the
forest (credit Sumatran Orangutan
Conservation Project)

Deforestation (credit Tim Bartley)

Palm Oil Plantation

Wildlife Protection Units (credit Peter Pratje)

Speaking Out For Orangutans

Volunteers

Rescued Orphan
Orangutan

Eco Tour Borneo

Habitat Destruction

demonstrate his understanding and awareness of his own mind and the possible desires of those of his orangutan family and friends.

Hsing Hsing and Nicole...

Perhaps this final brief story about Hsing Hsing shows not only his appreciation and awareness of others, but also his innate preference for redheads!

When we had to keep the orangutans inside within their relatively confined and unstimulating night quarters, we used to give them out of date women's magazines to keep them occupied and entertained. They would leaf through the pages, look at the pictures and generally find some interest in the images. However it was Hsing Hsing's behaviour with these magazines which both amused and amazed me. Because, without fail, Hsing Hsing used to tear out all of the pictures of Nicole Kidman and keep them as images of his favourite pin up girl. We even reciprocated by sticking these pictures to one wall of his night enclosure, which he appreciated. Of course this was in the early days when Nicole was a vibrant red head with lustrous curly long locks of hair and she certainly captured Hsing Hsing's attention.

Comprehension of Language and Communication

Even though orangutans don't have vocal chords to speak as we do, they are more than capable of learning sign language and understanding language as a means of communication with humans. We know that they can learn more than 200 words in American Sign Language and I have seen them comprehend spoken languages such as English and Indonesian. So they can communicate with us and we can literally have a conversation with them.

Of course they also have their own well developed form of communication with body language and to a lesser extent sounds which they use when interacting closely with other orangutans. These include kiss-squeaks and the long calls, which they send out into the forests to signal their presence in the environment. Orangutans utilise body language and non-verbal signals to communicate and exhibit many socially learned behaviours and cultural traditions which are passed down from generation to generation.

Chantek... the Orangutan Who Talks with Humans...

In addition to this, the example of Chantek, the orangutan who literally went to college and learned American Sign Language, is a perfect illustration of the capabilities of orangutans to learn and comprehend human language and communication. Reputedly he has mastered and used between150 to 200 hand symbols and gestures of sign language to communicate with his keepers and still demonstrates this talent to this day. Chantek also understands spoken English and responds to requests and commands as well as being able to point to, show and use objects to help his keepers understand what he is "talking about or referring to." [14]

Excellent Spatial Memory and Recognition of Events and People Over Time...

Orangutans also tend to have excellent memories in relation to the location of things and a capacity for remembering events and people over time. Not only do they need to learn and remember over 1,000 different edible foods within their forest home they also need to recall where to locate them. Therefore their ability to memorise elements within their surroundings and the specific locations of objects has most likely evolved due to their need to remember the position of food sources and fruiting trees within their jungle habitat across large areas of forest. They would also need to recall the specific timing of seasonal fruit becoming available at different stages throughout the year. So the capacity to recall such detailed knowledge of their local environment would serve to support their ongoing survival in the wild.

Furthermore it is thought that an orangutan's good memory for events and other beings would assist them to recognise and maintain good relationship with neighbouring orangutans within their territories. Orangutan keepers have also observed that they are capable of recognising and remembering people they have known and interacted with many years earlier. I have experienced this circumstance myself with both captive and wild born orangutans.

Some Memories Never Leave...

Mawas, the female orangutan who you have already met through some of her earlier escapades, and her fascinating personal history, illustrates how some memories can not only stay for a life time, but can also deeply impact our orangutan cousins. Mawas was originally a captive orangutan from the Sultan of Johor's personal collection and in her youth had lived through the 1942 World War II Battle of Singapore between the British and the Japanese. Being only a young orangutan at the time, Mawas had been terrified by the sounds and after-shocks of the intense bombing raids during this historic battle. Even though she was resettled in Perth Zoo, she continued to display adverse reactions to loud noises resembling the sounds of bombs.

Unfortunately, Perth Zoo is in close proximity to the South Perth river foreshore, which is the location of the annual Australia

Day fireworks display held on the 26th of January each year. So every Australia Day until her death, I would sit with Mawas as the fireworks exploded in the distance to reassure and comfort her from the frightening memories which were still triggered by those sounds. In Mawas's mind she was terrified that she was being bombed again.

Mawas died at age 58 as the oldest orangutan in captivity, at that time.

Orangutans are Persons...

By 1999, I had not only completed my studies, but a number of key events had occurred both within my personal and professional life which would result in me making some big changes, that were to have far reaching effects on my life into the future...

In 1998, I had made my decision to found and build an organisation which would work for the welfare, care and survival of all wild orangutans. So I formed The Orangutan Project and enrolled a number of my staff, and other dedicated individuals, to join the original team. Because I was still employed at the zoo, I was raising funds and working with the charity on a part time basis. Therefore we started in a small way, but always had a big vison for the charity and at least I felt as if we were taking some meaningful action on behalf of the orangutans which we supported.

The following year, Wendy and I got married. With a trip to the USA already booked we tied the knot in Las Vegas in front of an Elvis Presley impersonator at the Silver Bell Chapel in downtown Vegas. As a fitting honeymoon we proceeded to have a driving holiday around the USA, followed by going back packing around Europe. In addition to this, we had a two month stay at Apenheul Zoo, in The Netherlands, where I did some work as a primate keeper and advisor. Prior to arriving at the zoo, I had already helped them with design advice when they were planning their new orangutan exhibit and was asked to help settle some new orangutans in when they arrived. We were also fortunate enough to be given an apartment at the zoo just above the gorilla's night quarters, so whilst I worked, Wendy and I also enjoyed the sights and sounds of the picturesque Dutch countryside. I had definitely met my human red headed match, in Wendy.

Finally, by this stage, I had come to the inescapable conclusion that orangutans are actually persons. And I realised that if others didn't appreciate they were dealing with a person when they were relating with an orangutan, then there certainly would be a lack of understanding and a-disconnect when communicating with ,them. Therefore I appreciated that my task was not only to raise funds for orangutans, but also to educate people to the fact that orangutans were worthy of being recognised as persons and everything that entailed. This included the fact that they deserved to be cared for with the same dedication which we show to human children and they also have rights, even though they are not the same species as us. This shift in my perspective was one which for me began to pose an ethical question, because if I thought that orangutans should have rights, how could I reconcile keeping them in zoos?

This was a question which was to trouble me for a number of years, however at the time I had other things to focus my attention upon. As I was soon to receive the news that my great friend and mentor, Reg Gates, had died in difficult circumstances.

Reg's Death...

I was at home one morning and I received a call from Reg's wife Dianne. She was very upset and had called to say that Reg had been found dead in his car. I was so shocked, that after I hung up the phone, I actually started to think that I must have misheard Dianne and that this couldn't possibly be true. So I quickly rang up one of the other keepers just to check what Dianne had said and confirm that I was not somehow mistaken.

Unfortunately, I was not. Feeling deeply upset at the news of Reg's unexpected death, I did not trust myself to drive. So I asked my wife to take me to the zoo so I could tell the other staff, first hand, that our friend Reg was gone. The team was understandably as shocked and upset as I was…But the question on everyone's mind was, *"How could this have happened?"*

Unfortunately I knew that prior to this Reg had been finding it increasingly difficult to handle things at work. He was caught between an inability to cope with the situation and his unwillingness to abandon his staff and the animals under his care. It was a difficult time for all of us. But I had never dreamed that we may lose Reg, and the question haunted me, *"Could I have done more for my friend?"* It was a painful and heart wrenching experience in my life, however it was now my task to pick up the pieces and carry on without my trusted mentor.

At Reg's funeral, I recall silent tears sliding down my face as we slowly carried Reg's coffin up to the front of the room before it slid away to be cremated. Afterwards one of the zoo managers commented that he was surprised to see my tears flowing as they had, because he only knew me as a tough relentless animal advocate and union representative for my co-workers. But I guess what he did not understand was, why I always fought so hard for causes in which I believed. Because the only motivation I ever had was I actually cared for, and felt deeply about, the suffering of others and this was what always drove me forward.

CHAPTER 6
HOW SHOULD WE TREAT OUR
ORANGUTAN COUSINS?

"The assumption that animals are without rights and the illusion
that our treatment of them has no moral significance is a positively
outrageous example of western crudity and barbarity. Universal
compassion is the only guarantee of morality."
Arthur Schopenhauer

Knowing what I now knew about orangutans' level of self-awareness, reasoning skills and innate intelligence, as well as their ability to communicate and connect with humans, I consequently considered my orange friends as persons. Combined with my deeper understanding of them as living beings, I had also spent a number of years researching what could be done to improve their circumstances in captivity. From this vantage point, and my new position at the zoo as Curator of Primates, then Supervisor of Primates and eventually Exotics Curator, my priority turned towards protecting and defending their inalienable rights to live free of mental and physical suffering both in captivity and in the wild. Importantly, as they couldn't speak on their own behalf, I felt that this was what I needed to do.

It seemed that everything I had done up until this time had brought me to this point and it was my moment to stand up for what I knew was fair and just. Reg had shown me the importance of committing to my passion and to doing the right thing, even if it wasn't necessarily the most convenient thing to do personally. With his passing, I could see that in many ways he had passed the baton on to me. In fact I had founded The Orangutan Project, very much along the lines of Reg's own charitable foundation, The Silvery Gibbon Project. So I knew that the team at The Orangutan Project had much work to do with improving the welfare and rights of all orangutans, especially now I knew just how precarious their situation was in the wild, and how untenable it was for them to be kept in captivity.

Increasingly I wondered to myself, how we as humans could go on inflicting so much pain and suffering on orangutans? To me it simply did not make sense. I appreciated they were intelligent sentient beings who deserved to be treated with respect and care and to live freely in their environments in peace and safety. The problem was how to get the idea of human rights for orangutans not only be understood and accepted widely, but also embraced by those individuals who could actually do something about it?

Orangutans Deserve Human Rights…

"All truth passes through three stages.
First, it is ridiculed. Second, it is violently opposed.
Third, it is accepted as being self-evident."
Arthur Schopenhauer

As many of the world's great thinkers have said, ideas which question or run contrary to prevailing thought are often initially met with opposition and incredulity before being accepted. So you can imagine the idea of human rights for orangutans could be seen as *a stretch* for even some of the more open minded and even those who see themselves as animal lovers. However when you consider that it was less than 250 years ago, in 1776, that the founding fathers of the United States of America signed the Declaration of Independence.

A document which laid down the philosophy that all citizens were equal and entitled to specific inalienable rights including life, liberty and the pursuit of happiness. The contradiction here being that the majority of the signatories to the Declaration of Independence, which stated that it is self-evident that all people were equal in their newly independent land, also owned and used slaves as their personal property. In addition to this, these same founding fathers also kept their wives -the persons who raised their children and shared their beds- without rights to vote or possess property of their own. So it was as if the creators of a document, recognised as being ahead of its time, were in some ways blind to the contradictions it highlighted in their own lives. [15]

Therefore for those who hear that an orangutan deserves to have human rights and think it is strange, could consider that it is no-more *strange* than if we look back at those times when people of a different colour or sex had less rights than the ruling white male members of their own species. The point to remember here is that the people who thought like this only a few short centuries ago, and who behaved in ways in which today we would now view as unthinkable, were not uneducated slobs or unaware people of that time. Actually, quite the reverse was true, as the founding fathers were considered to be leaders in their field and the cream of the crop of great thinkers and statesmen of their era. So if they could have thought this way only such a short time ago perhaps it is time for us to re consider the way we see the rights of animals also?

Interestingly, it actually took almost another century for Abraham Lincoln to issue the Emancipation Proclamation in 1883, which legally freed all slaves in the rebellious Southern States of America during their hard fought, bloody Civil War...and this was less than 150 years ago. For American women their right to vote was not passed until 1919 and ratified in 1920 which is less than 100 years ago. This, in hindsight, seems quite an incredible fact to consider.

In regards to Australia, its record in terms of human rights has been a disappointing one of discriminatory restrictions against its indigenous population, the Aboriginals, who were not completely recognised as citizens until as late as 1962. Furthermore, women were unable to vote within Australia until South Australia permitted their vote in 1894, with the rest of the Australian states finally following suit in 1901. [16]

So perhaps it is time for all of us to expand our thoughts and open our minds to an idea whose time has come, that of human rights for orangutans and all Great Apes? And to make this change sooner rather than later?

Why Work For the Rights and Welfare of Orangutans?

For me it all comes down to the concepts of *consciousness, sentience* and the ability to *experience suffering....*

Consciousness...

One thing we all are aware of is that we are conscious. Without consciousness we could not feel pain or pleasure, hope or fear. However, many scientists still refuse to attribute consciousness to animals, as they reason that there can be no proof of the fact. On the surface of things, this is true, but what these scientists don't realise is that, in truth, they don't actually know if any other human being, other than themselves, *is conscious.* So the question is: *Why then do they assume that other human beings are conscious?* No doubt, this is because other human beings both act like them and react similarly to them...so they assume that other humans must be like them.

This, in fact, is a scientifically sound way of approaching the issue. Scientific method dictates that we shall assume that two things are alike unless they are proven different. So the question becomes then: *Why don't many scientists extend the assumption of consciousness to animals, especially the Great Apes who are so similar to humans in behaviour?*

I believe there are two reasons. Firstly, it is not generally perceived to be in the interests of scientists to assume consciousness in Great Apes because this would imply they have rights. Secondly, they have a lack of empathy for the Great Apes. Most importantly, empathy is needed to correctly interpret and understand any human or Great Ape because it means the ability to look at the world from another's point of view.

Some people believe that the presence of thinking or thought is proof of consciousness. In part this is true. But, we are aware of our thoughts. Therefore we are not our thoughts. We, the conscious principle or the inner observer, appear to be beyond our thoughts. So we come to the conclusion that there is no scientific way of knowing whether any animal or human, other than ourselves, is conscious, or like us, has the capacity to suffer. But, we don't necessarily have to stop our search here.

Basically, there are three methods from which we can gain knowledge; direct experience, inference and tradition. We have already exhausted the first two, so I will explore the third.

Certainly in most Eastern traditions consciousness is used as the most accurate description of *God* or the animating force of life. And it is this conscious principle or animating energy which is reflected in all living creatures. On the other hand, in the Western tradition, we see God speaking to Moses, saying "*I am that I am.*" Jehovah, stated as the true name of God in the Bible, means *I am.* Jesus said the "*kingdom of heaven is within you*". All indicating God is consciousness or the feeling of 'simply being' and it is God who is reflected in all humans as the conscious principle *I am.*

So what about animals? Geneses 25 says, *"And God made the beast of the earth according to its kind..."* Then Genesis 26 says, *"Then God said let Us make man in Our likeness..."* The interesting part here is that God suddenly becomes plural. That is the, *I am* of God was reflected in the beasts, just as in Hinduism and Buddhism, so surely we can assume here that this consciousness extends to all living beings also?

Therefore, if it is of our own direct experience that at least one creature is conscious, isn't it more sound to infer that, like ourselves, other creatures are also conscious...as our traditions appear to support this reasoning also? So logically, the next question becomes: *If all animals are conscious, why put the emphasis on Great Apes and more specifically, orangutans?* This is because, essentially the presence of consciousness in itself does not necessarily lead to suffering.

Suffering....

I'll explain the distinction around suffering with an example. We have all likely had the experience of watching terrifying events or confronting images in a movie, but when we come out of the movie theatre we are unaffected. We may even say that we enjoyed the movie. Why could we experience enjoyment when the events in the movie were so disturbing? The reason is that the mere witnessing, or being conscious of the events, does not directly lead to suffering. Because, in order to suffer, we need to be somehow attached to the events which occur around us.

For example if a friend's possessions are stolen we can all be philosophical and relatively detached about the situation. However, if the same event happened to us, we would most likely experience a degree of suffering. The difference is that we generally need to be *identified with* or *attached to* something before it can deeply affect us. This is the meaning of the metaphor of eating the apple from the tree of knowledge in the Bible. Before eating the apple, man was just conscious, but that consciousness or witnessing, was not identified with the body, and therefore did not suffer with the body. After eating the apple, however, man saw he *was the body*, symbolised by him knowing that he was naked. Now he was doomed to suffering, symbolised by his expulsion from the Garden of Eden.

So basically, in order for suffering to occur two things need to be present. Firstly consciousness has to be present, for example we don't suffer pain during surgical operations as we are usually rendered unconscious prior to the operation. Secondly the consciousness has to identify itself with its mind/body, and we as humans identify ourselves with our own bodies, as the physical vehicle which *houses us*.

From the information we covered in Chapter 5, we know that for most animals we can't irrefutably prove that their consciousness identifies itself with their bodies. On the other hand, we also can't know for sure that their consciousness doesn't. But we can be certain of this with some Great Apes, in particular, the orangutans. This has been illustrated by two well-known examples. As already discussed, orangutans can identify themselves in mirrors and photos, and if you put a dot of paint on their foreheads, then show them a mirror, orangutans will know that the dot is on themselves and they will reach for the offending mark. This is because they know they are conscious and they identify that consciousness with their bodies. In addition to this, there is also a large collection of evidence to show that orangutans can see the point of view of others and recognise this view point can be different from their own, demonstrating Theory of Mind.

Sentience....

Furthermore, orangutans are sentient beings. Sentience literally meaning:

"The capacity to feel, perceive, or experience subjectively. Eighteenth-century philosophers used the concept to distinguish the ability to think (reason) from the ability to feel (sentience)....In Eastern philosophy, sentience is a metaphysical quality of all things that requires respect and care." [17]

Remember the idea of orangutans being able to have their own subjective experience and to respond with feeling was raised as far back as Charles Darwin's observation of Jenny in London Zoo. And I have certainly personally witnessed the psychological and physical suffering of orangutans and their sentient responses. However, my experience of the grief of a mother orangutan for her dead child, and its impact upon the entire orangutan zoo colony, is perhaps one of the clearest demonstrations of sentience I can recall.

Puteri and Udara's Story...

Puteri was one of the most affectionate and physically demonstrative adult female orangutans within the Perth Zoo's colony. There was nothing more that Puteri loved than to be hugged and cuddled during contact sessions. As a mother, she was equally affectionate and caring with her young. At the time of this incident, Puteri had given birth to her daughter Udara as part of the zoo's breeding program. Udara had some health problems, so at one stage I had hand-raised her and had slept over in the night quarters. However Udara was able to be returned to Puteri and, without a doubt, she was doing a wonderful job with raising Udara, who was by this stage, a 4.5 year old juvenile.

I remember one morning at the beginning of my shift, coming

into the keeper's section behind the orangutan's night quarters and entering the raceway. As soon as I entered the space, I knew that something was wrong, because all of the orangutans were behaving strangely. When I got to Puteri and Udara's night quarters enclosure, I found Udara was dead in their cage. Sitting with Udara and holding her lifeless body in her arms was a devastated Puteri. Apparently Udara had passed away during the night of congenital heart failure and Puteri had realised that her daughter was gone and would not let her deceased body out of her arms. In fact it took at least a few days before Puteri would leave her daughter's side or her night quarters.

Puteri was obviously experiencing deep grief and mourning and it was equally clear that the whole colony was upset and feeling part of the sudden loss also. As I had nursed Udara and had enjoyed the bond between Puteri, Udara and myself, I was also exceptionally sad for Puteri. To see her so bereft and inconsolable was a moving experience for all of the keepers. Much like any grieving human mother, Puteri took some time to come to terms with Udara's death and to recover her usually affectionate temperament.

Therefore, undoubtedly orangutans have the ability to feel and perceive their experiences subjectively and respond accordingly to what has occurred for them. It is the presence of sentience which is a core component of the argument for human rights for orangutans, because sentience is necessary for a being to experience suffering. I can only conclude that Puteri was definitely experiencing this with the death of her much loved daughter, Udara.

To summarise this point:

1. We know from intelligence tests that orangutans are the most intelligent beings on the planet, after humans, and they adapt to their environment by passing on culture through each generation.

2. The more intelligent the being the more it can appreciate the

apparent continuity of thoughts in the past, to the present and into the future. Thus forming the concept of an individual identity or 'ego' that is identified with this specific mind/body.

3. More importantly, this identity takes ownership of desires and expectations for the present and future, along with regrets of the past. Further increasing the scope of suffering from the physical to the psychological.

4. We also understand that orangutans are extremely patient, intelligent beings who are naturally very observant and inquisitive. As self-aware beings, orangutans are recognised as possessing consciousness, sentience and thus able to experience suffering.

Therefore, their drive to extinction in the wild is an individual story of horror, played over and over again on a scale that is hard to comprehend. Furthermore, as humans, also recognised as sentient, compassionate beings, how can we continue to:

a) Confine them against their will in the often soulless, monotonous zoo environment, at times, treated without understanding or respect by their keepers?

b) Allow them to be macheted, shot, poisoned or burnt alive as agricultural pests?

c) Permit female orangutans to be slaughtered, whilst their babies are forcibly removed to be sold as pets?

It is this reasoning which has led me to specifically concentrate my resources towards the relief of the suffering of orangutans. The fact that I believe that orangutans are the most intelligent of Great Apes, in itself, does not necessarily mean that they are more *important* than other living beings, but their intelligence increases their potential to suffer. As all Great Apes and, others species such as elephants, have the intelligence of at least self-aware human children, they should all have the right to be free from suffering and to be cared for with the same dedication as we show our young. Because as humane individuals, we would never consciously allow a human child to suffer in this way.

What Are We to Do?

As an imperative we must immediately put the emphasis on relieving and ultimately eliminating the suffering of all orangutans, wild and captive. By focussing upon the reduction of suffering, this necessarily encompasses conservation, as the protection of their natural habitat greatly reduces their rate of suffering. On the other hand, conservation does not necessarily encompass the reduction of suffering of orangutans in captivity. There are many utilitarian reasons to conserve orangutans and the rainforests in which they live, however, if we concentrate on working for the reduction of suffering in these species, as well as humans, we will most likely work towards the right solutions.

In addition to this, for all of us who love and respect orangutans as intelligent and self-aware beings, our job is to understand that it is within human-kind's best interests to extend human rights to, but not limited to, our orange cousins. The destruction of their habitat by unsustainable land clearing and agriculture is destroying the environmental services humans rely upon, and causes significant global warming, affecting the future of the entire planet. From a moral perceptive the measure of a society is in how it treats those at its mercy, those who are disadvantaged or disempowered, whether they may be the indigenous peoples, prisoners, refugees or animals. It is easy to treat those who are more powerful or influential than us with respect and care, especially if we deem it to be in our self-interest to do so. The key is in how we treat those who have no power, no high status position and no voice to speak out for themselves. It is our treatment of these beings which defines us as people.

Ultimately, it is a damning reflection upon us as individuals and society as a whole if we let a sentient species, such as the orangutans, become extinct in our life time. We will diminish ourselves, our future and that of the generations to come after us. Therefore we are the ones who are lessened as people in the end. Furthermore, for us to allow this travesty to occur on *our watch*, when we are aware of the situation and more than capable of addressing and solving it as a priority, is simply unconscionable.

Just as importantly it is widely recognised that, if a society and its individual citizens are concerned only with their own self-centred desires and goals then as a people, they tend to be unhappy. Think of the decay and breakdown of the great empires as they fell into arrogance and copious consumption, only to ultimately disintegrate because of their own excesses and loss of purpose. On the other hand, a person or society which can appreciate higher ideals and see a cause bigger than themselves, will tend to be happier. Therefore, we contribute best to others by helping them to care about something other than themselves which benefits the society as a whole.

Stepping Up and Speaking Out...

With these ideals firmly within my mind I began to look for ways to bridge the gap between ending suffering for captive orangutans whilst using The Orangutan Project as a vehicle to fight for their rights in their natural habitat. The Perth Zoo was already recognised as a leader in its field in regard to the health and well-being of its orangutan colony. However, in 2001 we were able to push through with the commencement of major renovations to the outdated orangutan facilities. This involved a staged redevelopment to provide additional enclosures for the orangutans and new state of the art climbing structures and behavioural enrichment devices. The results being that over time the resident Perth Zoo orangutans were housed in what could only be described as the best captive facilities in the world. At least we were able to provide our orange cousins with conditions which were designed to not only reduce their suffering but also to increase their happiness, physical and mental well-being.

On the other side of things, by the mid 2000's, I had begun working upon an audacious, ground breaking plan to release a zoo born orangutan back to her wild habitat. It was something which had never been attempted before and which many said could never be achieved. However, the nay-sayers had not met our number one orangutan candidate, a super intelligent, fiery red headed Sumatran female orangutan named, Temara. Nor did they understand the commitment and dedication of the team behind this world first plan, which included the Head Orangutan Keeper, Kylie Bullo. So the scene was set for a step forward into the realm of making the seemingly impossible, possible.

Temara's Journey to Freedom...

In order to properly describe Temara's journey and to fully appreciate its potentially far reaching impacts for all captive orangutans, it's important to know her background.

Temara's grandmother, Puan, was originally a wild born orangutan who, as a baby, saw her mother killed by her captors. Ultimately, she was held in Johor Zoo, where sadly she was probably not well treated by her keepers. From there, Puan was sent to Perth Zoo in 1968. As part of the breeding program in Perth Zoo, Puan gave birth to Temara's mother, Puteri. (You have already been introduced to

Puteri as the highly affectionate female orangutan in her story about Udara.) Temara was born to Puteri in September 1992, and from the time of her birth, Temara always demonstrated that she had a mind and a will of her own. As she grew up under the loving, watchful care of Puteri, Temara was to increasingly display her strong, independent and, on many occasions, characteristically fiery temperament. In short Temara was not only easily led astray, she also was quick to learn new habits…both the good, but mostly the bad, which served to make life for her patient mother and her exasperated keepers more than interesting!

However, what made Temara particularly suitable for this mission, was the fact that at the zoo, we always concentrated on building loving personal relationships with the orangutans within our care. I had already formed a solid relationship with Temara's mother, Puteri, and had also helped to raise Temara, so she had a well-established, loving and respectful relationship with myself and the team. Which meant that Temara knew us well and we relied upon this fact because we knew that she would respond to us if we needed her to come down from the trees to be checked once she had been released into the wild. On the other hand, Temara was also well suited for release because she never really liked humans per-se, so she wouldn't actively pursue contact with them after her release. This meant that she would be less likely to put herself into harm's way by willingly interacting with unknown humans who may well wish to hurt her. Finally, she was both physically and mentally fit, exceptionally intelligent and naturally independent, therefore Temara met all of the criteria to be selected for a program of this kind.

Knowing all of these factors about Temara, we then developed a program to enhance and enrich the following areas:

1. Physical health
2. Mental health

3. Social health
4. The strength and depth of her knowledge of forest survival skills.

This was because what's missing in most young orangutans housed in rescue centres in Sumatra and Borneo is their mental health. As this is the aspect which is most easily destroyed when they have not only seen their mothers slaughtered, but they have also missed the nurturing childhood experience of being raised by them. The result being they are, quite frankly, emotionally abused and therefore *behind the eight ball* in reaching the next stage of their natural development.

A young male orangutan, named Tatok, who was at one of the release sites supported by The Orangutan Project, was a clear example of this. He displayed all of the hallmarks of an emotionally abused individual. In jungle school he would sit on the forest floor, refusing to interact with either his peers or the centre's technicians. Instead he would simply sit in a corner rocking backwards and forwards like a child with mental health issues would do. Therefore we knew that Tatok lacked mental health but felt that we could do something to assist him and change his life for the better. So through The Orangutan Project I sent Kylie, the experienced, skilled and naturally talented Head Orangutan Keeper from Perth Zoo and The Orangutan Project's Project Manager, up to the rescue centre to work with Tatok for six weeks.

As a member of the early team of The Orangutan Project, Kylie committed to do this work whilst on her annual leave. So over that intensive and personally challenging six week period, Kylie worked with Tatok and showered him with the love, affection and empathy which he so sorely needed. In addition to this Kylie also worked dedicatedly with Tatok to help him to learn how to search for food, build his own night nest and generally re-adjust to the possibility of re-release into the wild. Remarkably Tatok responded exceptionally well and was ultimately released back into his natural forest environment. For us, we had demonstrated that we could work with an orangutan who was not in good mental health and turn his prospects for the future around through a caring and nurturing approach...and Tatok proved it was possible.

Back at the zoo, we knew that for orangutans, as with humans, for them to be confident, secure and happy adults they needed a loving and secure environment in which to grow up. We also knew that those individuals who have had the most nurturing and loving environment in childhood are the ones who succeed the best out in the wild. Temara had received all of this as a foundation because she was raised well and under the constant care of her loving mother Puteri.

From that time forward we began to work with Temara to prepare her as much as we could for her history making journey into her natural habitat. Firstly we had a real tree made available for use with Temara within Perth Zoo and we allowed her to feed from this tree. To mimic the conditions we would have to employ within the forest, we would then call her down from the top of the tree so that we could check on her. From then on we began speaking to her in Indonesian so she became familiar with the words which both, we and her Indonesian support team, would be using in the field. In addition to this, when we took her back to her night quarters we fed her with foods similar to those she would need to be able to identify and source within the wild. So there was a large amount of preparation for Temara to undertake before she even left the zoo.

Once we considered her ready, Kylie and I made the arduous journey with Temara to her natural forest environment in 2006. Once there, we began intensively working with her at a release site in Sumatra, run by my friend Peter Pratje from the Frankfurt Zoological Society.

Temara literally had to go through Jungle Orientation Classes

101 and be able to demonstrate her understanding and proficiency with sourcing, collecting and consuming natural jungle foods before she would be considered ready to be independent in the forest. She also needed to show that she could locate a suitable tree within which to construct her own night nest each evening in her future life of freedom. With Kylie there on the ground for a total of three months, she was able to supervise Temara and oversee her training and ultimately her successful release into the wild. Together we had achieved the unthinkable and taken a zoo born captive orangutan and set her free back into her natural habitat. (And if you would like to read the inspiring full story of this event, I recommend that you get yourself a copy of Kylie's heart-warming book covering Temara's journey, *"Reaching for the Canopy"* which I recommend in the *Further Reading* section of the book)

Now, from Temara's remarkable story a number of beneficial outcomes occurred.

Importantly, because it was a project undertaken by the Perth Zoo and in conjunction with the Indonesian government, the Frankfurt Zoological Society and The Orangutan Project, it was necessarily a highly publicised and widely reported event. The idea of putting an Australian, captive born orangutan back into the wild was a unique and newsworthy event and it therefore captured the attention of both politicians and the media within both countries. We therefore attracted the attention of ministers, ambassadors, and public figures within each country.

More importantly Temara and her journey to freedom became a symbol and a constant reminder of the importance of the protection of orangutan habitat, especially the Bukit Tigapuluh ecosystem where she now lives. So perhaps Temara had done more than any orangutan had ever done for the survival of her species. In that, this single and remarkable orangutan had not only improved her quality of life within the forest, she had also highlighted the need for all orangutans to live free and safe within their protected natural habitat.

You will be happy to hear that this was not the last time that I would see and interact with my fiery red headed orangutan friend, Temara. Because our next encounter would be one which would touch and move me in a way that I could not have imagined at the time of her ground breaking release…but I will share this story with you later within the book.

From this point onwards, things were becoming a little more complicated for me as I was often both the spokesperson for the Perth Zoo and also The Orangutan Project and our aims were clearly moving further and further apart from each other. I was beginning to speak out publicly about my opposition to orangutans being kept captive within zoos and this obviously was becoming an issue for both myself and the zoo's management. It was nearly time for me to take another step further along my path. However, I loved the orangutans at Perth Zoo and did not wish to leave them and felt torn with the thought of moving away from these beings whom I had come to know and love.

Yet, as I said at the beginning of this book, life has a way of putting major choices before us and it is always our responsibility as to how we will respond. Soon life would do just that and my choice would change the course of my life once more.

SECTION 3

THE ORANGUTAN PROJECT:
STEPPING OUT AND STANDING UP

*"To spend one's life being angry and in the process doing
nothing to change it, is to me ridiculous.
I could be mad all day long, but if I'm not doing a
damn thing, what difference does it make?"*
Charles Fuller

CHAPTER 7
COMPASSION, PROTECTION,
FREEDOM.

*"You never change things by fighting the existing
reality, to change something, build a new model
that makes the existing model obsolete."*
R. Buckminster Fuller

By 2009 I had been Curator of Exotics at the Perth Zoo for eight years and, up until this time, I had been able to work on a part time basis within The Orangutan Project and manage the two quite well. However, due to my increasingly outspoken stance on the inappropriateness of keeping self-aware sentient beings, such as orangutans, in captivity, combined with my inner conflict about being a part of the very system I questioned, I realised that my time at the zoo was coming to an end. The biggest problem for me was how could I leave my orangutan friends and simply walk away? Because there was one thing which I knew about myself and that was…I don't give up on those I love easily or quickly.

On the other hand there was a larger and more pressing issue at play and a purpose much bigger than my own personal attachments. That was the impending extinction in the wild of the critically endangered Sumatran orangutans and the very real possibility that the, already endangered, Bornean orangutans would follow suit. So the choice for me came down to the simple fact that I could stay at the zoo and ensure that my captive friends were kept as mentally and physically healthy as possible, and continue working with those I loved, which *felt good in the short term*. Or, conversely, I could turn my attention to and invest my time and energy full time into working on the bigger picture, ensuring the survival of these two species. No doubt, the latter was the more challenging path to take. However it was the only choice with the potential to create the one result which would most benefit the orangutans and ultimately create the greatest *good in the long term* ... to save these majestic beings from extinction.

And as Reg had taught me so many years earlier, the demonstration of an individual's commitment is in doing the right thing even when it isn't personally convenient or necessarily easy to do so. Nevertheless, I had a little more work to do before I was ready to leave the zoo, and part of this was to visit an old friend of mine in Bukit Tigapuluh, Sumatra.

Meeting Temara, Wild and Free...

Since Temara's release back into the wild three years earlier, she had been regularly monitored by a Frankfurt Zoological Society team, as well as six monthly visits from myself or other members of my team to ensure that she was not only surviving in her new home, but also thriving. We had kept a close eye on our pioneering orangutan friend and knew that she was doing well living wild and free. This was good news for all of us at the zoo and, in particular, Kylie and I were overjoyed to have successfully demonstrated that a release of this kind was not only possible, but could now be repeated in the future.

In 2009, I was on one of the inspection visits into the jungle near Temara's release site at Bukit Tigapuluh and was keen to see if I could closely inspect my independent friend in her new home. As soon as I arrived at the release site, I headed out into the area of forest where Temara had most recently been observed. I was filled with both anticipation and a calm excitement at the prospect of seeing her once again. From my perspective, to see her living in her natural environment thousands of kilometres away from her captive birth place in Perth Zoo, would be reward enough for all of the work it had taken to achieve this result. As I walked along the narrow forest path with its densely treed surroundings, I called out her name and looked up towards the canopy in search of any signs of Temara. Memories of this remarkable orangutan flooded my thoughts. We had shared so many experiences together and she had always been a non-conformist at heart who made her feelings known to all in her immediate vicinity. I pondered just how far she had come to ultimately arrive at this point.

Suddenly in the trees above I saw movement and a flash of the familiar vibrant signature orange colour of an adult Sumatran orangutan's body hair. Straining my neck to get a better view, I looked upwards and saw Temara's inquisitive, cheeky face peering down at me from her treetop sanctuary. In that moment we looked at each other and I saw recognition in her eyes, I couldn't help but smile back at her in heart felt greeting. We held each other's gaze for a few more moments and then Temara began to move. The question was, what would this independent and unpredictable being do next?

With ease and grace Temara began to move expertly down the trunk of the tree in which she was feeding and positioned herself to within an arms-length of where I was standing at the base of the tree. Grasping the trunk with one hand, she slowly extended out her other hand towards me. In response, I reached up to her and we were able to hold each other's hand in the forest for some time. Temara silently holding onto her tree and me standing mutely in awe and wonder at what was occurring. Soon Temara would be interested in the supplementary food that I would give her to reward her for allowing me to inspect her teeth, hair and body fat, however for a moment holding my hand was the priority. For me, it was a recognition and a greeting, but more than that, it was a sign that we knew and respected each other as conscious beings. We were able to have this connection with each other for a brief moment and for me it was a very special event.

Here I was connecting with and relating to an orangutan who was totally wild and free, an orangutan for whom there was no necessity at that moment to do so. Instead she was acting out of choice and free will, because she was able to acknowledge our relationship on her own terms and on her own turf. To meet with Temara once again under these circumstances was perhaps one of the most precious and poignant experiences I have ever had. Strangely enough, it was one for which words seem somehow inadequate to describe its impact and beauty…I can only say, what was present in this experience was the essence of love, in the greatest sense of the word.

Just as importantly, however, the successful release of Temara and her new life in the forest meant the realisation of a number of key milestones for me as a conservationist for orangutans:

Firstly, it clearly demonstrated that through my time at the Perth Zoo, I had been able to continue on with the great work that people like Charlie Broomfield, Rosemary Markham and Reg Gates had championed all those years back. And I only wished that these remarkable persons could have been here to see just how far we had come.

Secondly, I had been able to research, oversee and implement a range of improvements to the captive orangutan's zoo environment and care practices.

Thirdly, it showed that our team had been able to plan and execute a project involving a captive born orangutan's release back to her home habitat. Furthermore, we'd been able to introduce the idea that one day more of the zoo's colony could also be released to live wild and free. (To date this has enabled Perth Zoo to allow two more orangutans, Semaru and Nyaru, to make the journey from the zoo to the wild.)

And finally, there was one last area in which the Exotics Section had made great progress and that was in the area of its team of staff.

Passing the Baton Forward…

By this stage, we'd been able to make some great leaps forward with the employment of a diverse and talented range of individuals. For example, unlike back in the 1980's when I was first employed, the zoo was no longer the domain of predominantly male zookeepers. In fact within the Primate Section, in particular, I had been able to select and employ many enthusiastic and high calibre women, such as Kylie Bullo and Clare Campbell. I had noticed with interest that, generally, these young women brought a particular kind of understanding and compassion to their work for the primates and functioned well as a cohesive team. So the previous culture of the "hunter and man-handlers" of animals had well and truly passed away.

In addition to this, our new candidates were usually degree educated biologists or similarly qualified, which meant that they demonstrated the insight and knowledge that either a biological or environmental science graduate possesses due to their depth of study. They also usually possessed an aptitude for their chosen profession, plus an innate affinity with the natural world because they wanted to *work for animals* instead of just *with them*. Often passionate environmentalists and conservationists the new keepers and supervisors were committed to the welfare of the primates first and foremost. Therefore they were interested in developing and introducing improved practices and behavioural enrichment, instead of avoiding them. So in many ways, both the primates in their care and the zoo as a whole, benefitted. As you can imagine, this was a world away from my early employment days, when I was seen as a risky experiment specifically *due to* my qualifications.

Furthermore, I had also been able to develop and promote new and upcoming staff on the basis of merit rather than via the previous system of seniority. Under the system of seniority it was almost as if, as long as you did your time, you were going to be rewarded with promotion... no matter how incompetent you were. This had obvious drawbacks for any team, so I chose to change this old framework. To do this we rewarded talent and skill with promotion which meant that individuals were no longer promoted based upon the years of service they had completed, but rather on their suitability for the position. This immediately levelled the playing field and allowed me to choose the best people available. My rationale was that if you believed in a cause that was important to you, you will choose people better than you, or with different skills from your own. More importantly, by recognising those with talent and moving them upwards I could create a team which was made up of individuals who were usually better, smarter and had different or complimentary skills to the existing team. It was a win-win all round.

However, as often happens when introducing change, it wasn't all smooth sailing and I recall a situation when I first became Curator of Exotics, back in 2001. At the time I had promoted a talented young keeper named Clare Campbell into the role of Supervisor of Primates. Unfortunately, for many of the old guard at the zoo, the problem was that she had only been with the zoo for around three years. In addition, I promoted her over a person who had 25 years of service. This choice ruffled a few feathers within the organisation and I received quite a bit of criticism for my choice. With someone even saying to me, "*How dare you do that.*" My only response to this was the truth, "*She's actually better suited and the best candidate for the position and I don't care how many years' experience someone has had... I just want the best person for the job and for the primates.*"

Therefore I pushed forward the creation of promotion based upon meritocracy rather than seniority within our team. To my mind, this ensured that we had the best possible group of people to work for all of the beings in our care. Because of this approach we had developed a culture of close knit and dedicated professionals. Most importantly, I knew that the team I would leave behind was a solid one which would carry on the work for the orangutans and other primates. It was time for me to pass the baton over to the next generation of primate keepers.

Sometimes You Just Need a Little Push....

In late 2011 I received an unwanted move to the newly created position as the Curator of Collections for the Perth Zoo. This position offered a higher salary and a better office but ultimately resulted in me having much less input and decision-making-power. It also made it harder for me to effect change on the ground both within the team and for the animals in their care. It was just the push I needed to step out and within two months I had made the choice to leave the Perth Zoo, after 27 years of service. I switched over to the position of CEO of The Orangutan Project, first on a part time basis for both The Orangutan Project and Wildlife Asia, then after a year, on a full time basis with The Orangutan Project in 2012.

My exit from the zoo was, in the end, a mutually agreeable one which benefitted both the zoo's management and myself for a number of reasons. Perhaps the most obvious ones being that the zoo no longer had to deal with my outspoken opposition to keeping orangutans in captivity. As well as handle my refusal to manage the Asian elephants due to my objections to the use of physical discipline on these intelligent and aware animals. On the other hand, at last I was totally free to commit all of my time and energy into The Orangutan Project to ensure the survival of orangutans in the wild. By this stage it was the purpose and the work most close to my heart.

A Fond Farewell...

In the days leading up to my departure, I spent as much time as I could with my orangutan friends. This meant that I arranged contact sessions in the orangutan enclosures with some of the females. As well as making sure that I had time to interact with my old friend Hsing Hsing and the other male, Dinar. It was my way of saying goodbye to these persons whom I had come to know and care deeply about during the more than two decades that I had been part of the zoo's primate team. The simple truth was that I loved these beings, and, although I knew it was time for me to move on to the bigger task of saving their species in the wild, I knew that I would miss them too.

On the last day, as I exited Puteri's exhibit, after one final hug with her, the Primate Section team swung into action with their own version of a leaving party. Firstly, they gave me the traditional farewell practice of *locking the keeper in the safety-raceway,* followed by a public soaking from the nearest hose. Saturated from head to toe and dripping wet, I was then treated to a large and heart felt farewell lunch with the entire crew. Which the wonderful team paid for from their own pockets. It was a fitting end to my zoo career and as I left the zoo for the last time, I silently sent both my human and orangutan friends a promise that I would do everything that I could to ensure the orangutans' place in the wild.

Dispelling Some Zoo Myths...

It is important for me to point out here that whilst I am not totally opposed to zoos in all cases and for all animals, it is definitely time for a different approach across the zoo industry. Furthermore, I think that it is vital to dispel a few of the myths which zoos currently perpetuate to protect and defend their existence. These being:

1. *The Ark Concept-* This is where zoos position themselves as the key vehicles for the protection and preservation of the species they hold. The problem with this idea is that most captive zoo mega fauna populations are not genetically viable, because they do not contain a large enough gene pool or the required genetic diversity to ensure the continuation of a species on their own. The truth is, zoo populations actually need to rely upon the constant introduction of new wild animals to provide the fresh genes they need to survive. There are often many issues with breeding animals in captivity due to the lower levels of mental and physical well-being amongst many of the animals. Therefore it is a falsity for zoos to present themselves as the *arks* of the world's species.

2. *Animal Longevity-* Another idea which is often given in support of zoos is that all animals live longer and are more likely to be healthy in captivity. However, this is also a false assertion and, depending on the species, often the reverse is true. For example, my Masters research showed that orangutans in zoos have life expectancies which are less than half of their free and wild relatives. After removing mortality in the first five years and restricting data to the last ten years, captive orangutans only lived on average to 12 years of age, compared to the likelihood of living well into their 60s for their wild counterparts. This is, no doubt in part due to the fact that a zoo is just not able to provide orangutans with the size of enclosure and the rich social environment which these aware and intelligent beings require. I can honestly say I have known animals to die in captivity *as a direct result* of the treatment and incorrect care they received within zoos.

3. *Happiness in Captivity-* There is a belief that somehow captive animals are just as happy in captivity as they are in

the wild. However, this myth denies the evidence that many captive animals demonstrate behaviours which have been termed as *stereotypic*. Which means that because of their captivity, animals are known to sometimes develop neuroses, depression and can even act in self harming ways. More specifically, as I have already said, my biggest issue with zoos had become the keeping of highly intelligent self-aware, sentient beings in captivity, including Great Apes and other animals such as elephants. This is because these beings have the greatest capacity to suffer under these circumstances and, in particular, it is the suffering experienced in captivity which is an undeniable abuse of their rights as persons to be able to live wild and free.

4. *Animal Welfare is #1-* Unfortunately the majority of zoos are run as public entertainment centres, therefore within the upper management there is a focus on the *business side of things* instead of the welfare of the animals. This also means that most CEOs of zoos are either business or marketing specialists or long standing public servants who lack an in-depth knowledge of animals or their care. It's not that they are bad or evil people, it's just that the values of animal welfare and conservation are not their first priorities. Thus, there is a mismatch within the organisation. With the often conflicting interests of operating an entertainment enterprise, catering for the needs and desires of the visiting public, as well as attempting to fulfil their purported organisational aims of education, research and conservation, the welfare of the captive animals can be low on the list of zoo priorities. In addition to this, it is recognised that an organisation is *what it measures,* so a zoo doesn't measure how much habitat it has saved or how many animals they have protected in the wild. Instead they measure indicators such as, if the public

was happy during their visit or if they have achieved their marketing and PR goals in the media and TV. Consequently, what a zoo appears to be or presents itself as doing from the outside, is not necessarily a true reflection of how it operates behind the scenes.

Therefore, after many years spent trying to change things within the zoo system for the betterment of the captive animals and their keepers, I think that it is time for a major change across the zoo industry. In fact, what is needed is a wholesale shift to a new paradigm and a fresh approach to the role which zoos could play on behalf of all animals. In my mind I can see that zoos could be very effective acting as a *shop front* or *access point* for real, measurable, on the ground conservation efforts. With their interface with the general public, perhaps there is a place for modern, forward thinking zoos of the future to actually contribute to the conservation of some animal species…but first the over-riding ethos of most zoos must change and until they do, there is a long way to go.

The Zoo as a Learning Ground…

However, to be fair to the Perth Zoo, although my years with them had not been without challenge, they gave me the perfect foundation on which to expand and build The Orangutan Project into the future. In fact, on reflection, my time there had helped to form much of who I have become as a person by exposing me to experiences and opportunities which I would never have otherwise encountered. Most importantly, my work with the zoo had instilled within me an iron clad determination to make a practical and lasting difference for all orangutans and other beings on the planet. It has also demonstrated to me the power of speaking up and taking direct action on their behalf. So for this alone I will always be appreciative.

Furthermore, as I reflect upon my time there, I can see a distinct set of other lessons which I was able to take with me.

Meeting the Orangutans....

Without a doubt, my introduction to the orangutan colony at the zoo has essentially shaped my working life. I had the privilege of working for the orangutans, and coming to know them as two distinct species of self-aware Great Apes. Both my studies and duties at the zoo meant I was able to research and learn about their behaviour and temperaments, first hand. On a personal level, I had formed loving and meaningful relationships with all of the orangutans with whom I worked. In addition to this, I had come to know their individual character and personality traits, much like humans get to know a group of close friends as they share life's events over time. Quite frankly, to me they were *family*.

Working with Great People...

In terms of the people I had closely worked with over those 27 years, they were, in the main a diverse and unique group of individuals who believed in the causes of animal welfare and conservation. I had been fortunate enough to take over care of the orangutans from the dedicated Primate Section Keeper Charlie Broomfield and work with his wife, respected orangutan researcher, Dr Rosemary Markham. I was also mentored by Reg Gates and had the honour of working alongside many other like-minded and talented colleagues. In the field of Primatology, my role at the zoo enabled me to meet and spend time with two of the three most famous primatologists of our time. Jane Goodall, known for her work with chimpanzees and Birute Galdikas, recognised for her pioneering work with orangutans. Unfortunately, the final member of their three women unit - known as "*The Trimates*"- the renowned gorilla advocate, Dian Fossey, had been killed during her work in the field in Africa. So I did not have the opportunity to meet with her, however I had the privilege of working with her student Ian Redman.

International Exposure...

I had also worked and collaborated with other captive orangutan specialists around the globe and had consulted with them on their planning and design of enclosures and behavioural enrichment techniques. This sometimes meant that I travelled internationally to a number of zoos and experienced, first hand, the diverse range of conditions under which orangutans were held. Furthermore, it was through the Perth Zoo and my work with The Orangutan Project that we had been able to devise and create Temara's history making release into the wild. Therefore all of these hands-on encounters provided me with priceless experience across a range of aspects within my field.

The Organisation...

In hindsight, I can also see that the very challenges I had faced at the zoo, as well as the successes I had been a part of along the way, had clearly shown me those values and structures which worked within an organisation...and those which didn't. As a consequence I learned from experience what not to do, as well as what to emulate. This learning was an integral part of the knowledge which I took with me into The Orangutan Project. It meant that we were able to create and build an organisation with the aim of looking after its people as well as its cause. Specifically, we wanted to improve the environment in which our team worked, and establish a place where good people were developed and nurtured, instead of being destroyed. This resulted in The Orangutan Project's team making some different choices when it came to how we worked together as an organisation and as individuals in the field.

And of course, a great benefit from my time at the zoo was that I had been able to initially grow The Orangutan Project gradually and consolidate our team, build a committed group of donors, supporters and volunteers, as well as develop a wide reaching network of orangutan conservation contacts. This meant that over the years we had already completed a number of successful and targeted projects within the field and were ready for a major step forward with our work.

The Orangutan Project, a Big Leap Forward…

Much like Temara, when I left the zoo environment, I was free to act without apology or censure. At last, I was *all in* with The Orangutan Project and it was time for me to step out onto the global arena in a more focussed way. By doing this I was able to take on the bigger job of leading the organisation forward so we could increase our work on behalf of all orangutans with greater urgency and on a larger scale. My energy was now solely directed towards doing all that I could to save orangutans from extinction and ensuring their long term survival in the wild. However, I could see that it was a race against time, because in Indonesia and Malaysia their natural habitat was being destroyed at an alarming rate and their position in the wild becoming even more tenuous…so it was the perfect opportunity for The Orangutan Project to take a big leap forward.

Working for orangutans with the three key principles of Compassion, Protection and Freedom, The Orangutan Project has always had a very clear directive which underpins all of our projects.

Compassion – This is the organisation's reason for being and our *why?* So we work to ensure orangutans' care, welfare and survival in all areas because we see them as persons, alongside the people.

Protection – This is *what* we do as an organisation and we act in many ways to protect orangutans in their wild habitat and those that have been forced into captivity.

Freedom – Ultimately, this is our core vision and *how* we see all orangutans living into the future, that they will be enabled to live meaningful lives as persons, wild, free and safe.

To carry out our vital work in the field for wild orangutans in Sumatra and Borneo and for captive orangutans around the globe, we follow three aims as a conservation charity and an active *on the ground* organisation.

1. **Raise Money**- Our focus on developing and growing our fund raising revenue is critical to The Orangutan Project, because without the all-important flow of funds for the cause, we will be unable to help the orangutans over the long term. It is vitally important to realise that we must be good at this, because we simply cannot miss a year in terms of fund raising. To do so would mean an area of habitat could suddenly become unprotected, causing all of our previous conservation work to be lost. Therefore we must be sustainable as an organisation, which makes our efforts to connect with and build a loyal, committed donor base vital to ensure an ongoing cash flow to fund our projects.

2. **Make Meaningful Change** – We use the money we raise as effectively as possible to support orangutans and create meaningful change for them on our donors' behalf. *And what is considered meaningful change?* As an organisation we know that we are what we measure. So our key performance measures are based upon our actual impact and performance in the field such as:

   • How much rain forest habitat have we secured and protected for the orangutans?

- How many orangutans have we helped to rescue, rehabilitate and release back into the wild?
- How many local communities have we worked with to help educate and support them with ongoing mutually beneficial projects?
- How have our lobbying and awareness efforts improved the circumstances for orangutans?

By measuring these indicators, The Orangutan Project can ensure that our work remains effective and relevant for all orangutans.

3. **Run Efficiently and Successfully** - Ultimately we aim to run efficiently and successfully as a fundraising charity, which means that we maintain low overheads whilst channelling our funds into worthy and effective projects. However, I think perhaps what makes The Orangutan Project different from others in the area is the way we advance our vision for the future.

Firstly, we are co-operative and collaborative, which means that we actively work with the existing orangutan conservation organisations which are achieving results for orangutans in the field. We work alongside them to amplify the results for our cause. For example, if there is already a well-respected orangutan rehabilitation centre in an area in which we work, instead of establishing another centre of our own, we will collaborate with the existing centre to support and improve their results. In this way we save precious funds and do not duplicate projects unnecessarily.

Secondly, our ultimate mission is *to not have to exist at all*. In fact we are striving as an organisation to reach a time when

The Orangutan Project is no longer needed and is rendered obsolete. When we have ensured the survival of orangutans and have them living free, safe and protected in the wild with vibrant and viable populations, our work will have been done...and this is the mission we all hold dear to our hearts.

However, for now we still have a long way to go with this mission and in the next chapter I'll share with you a couple of stories of the orangutans we have worked with which demonstrate just *what we do* and *why our work is so needed.*

CHAPTER 8
WHAT WE DO AND HOW WE DO IT

"Never doubt that a small group of thoughtful, committed citizens can change the world, indeed it is the only thing that ever has."
Margaret Mead

What We Do ….

Since our inception in 1998, The Orangutan Project has contributed in excess of $10 million directly into orangutan conservation and rehabilitation projects in the field…where it is urgently needed. Today, we are an innovative, dynamic and successful not-for-profit organisation which supports a wide range of projects vital to *addressing and solving* the major challenges facing orangutans in the wild.

The projects funded by The Orangutan Project not only include specific orangutan conservation, such as orangutan rescue, rehabilitation and release programs, but also habitat protection and regeneration, education, research, local community partnerships as well as, fighting deforestation and the loss of habitat at the highest levels.

Our unique focus upon tying funding to *direct outcomes* for orangutans has enabled us to work with the majority of bona fide orangutan conservation projects operating on the ground today in Borneo and Sumatra. This has resulted in bringing together key players and diverse conservation groups who work tirelessly in the field to ensure the orangutans' survival.

Importantly it has been The Orangutan Project's practical, collaborative and hands on approach which has greatly increased our ability to achieve measurable outcomes for orangutans and make inroads towards saving the species as a whole. In fact, through orangutan orphan *Adoption Programs*, regular donations and targeted appeals, we may have been able to achieve more for the species than *any other* single orangutan conservation group.

In addition to this, because of our highly focused and cost efficient work, we have earned a reputation amongst our partners and donors for being a financially responsible and transparent conservation organisation. This is demonstrated by the fact that 100% of all donated monies go straight into the field, whilst our overall administration costs are funded via non tax-deductible fundraising activities. It is in this way that we make sure that every dollar donated works on behalf of the orangutans we protect and support.

However, our long-term growth and sustainability has only been made possible through the loyal support of our individual donors and volunteers, many of whom have supported us each and every year since we began. Such ongoing physical and financial assistance is imperative for us to reach our goal of increasing the number of wild orangutans under The Orangutan Project's permanent protection. This will ensure sufficient numbers of each orangutan subspecies survives indefinitely.

In the 2015 / 2016 financial year alone, The Orangutan Project achieved the following results for orangutans and the local communities which live and work alongside them in Sumatra and Borneo.

Saving Orangutans

- ✓ 84 rescues of captive or injured orangutans
- ✓ 206 orangutans individually cared for
- ✓ 47 rehabilitated orangutans released back into the wild

Protecting Forest Habitat

- ✓ 332,000 hectares of forest protected
- ✓ 3,500 orangutans living within protected habitat areas

Building Community Support

- ✓ 6 orangutan caring scholarships
- ✓ 20 community development projects
- ✓ 100 schools and communities provided with education classes, with thousands of people being reached

Changing the Game

- ✓ Supporting 3 legal cases against deforestation
- ✓ 38,000 hectares of forest purchased
- ✓ Involved in scientific and community input of land use planning for 1.3 million hectares of threatened rain forest

With our consistent focus upon our Vision and Mission, we intend to continue to widen and expand our results to ensure that the currently fragmented orangutan populations, not only survive but will one day again thrive in their natural habitat.

Our Vision

That all orangutans will live in the wild, within secure, protected and viable populations.

Our Mission

To ensure the survival of both Sumatran and Bornean orangutan species in their natural habitat and promote the welfare of all orangutans.

To reach our aims into the future, our current Action Plan includes specific targets which we are working to achieve over the next ten years. These are as follows, to:

1. Increase the number of wild orangutans under permanent protection by The Orangutan Project to 8,000 individuals to ensure all distinct populations of orangutans survive indefinitely.
2. Secure 1,800 km² of prime lowland forest as sustainable orangutan habitat.
3. Protect these prime lowland forest areas with teams comprised of trained and active Wildlife Protection Rangers.
4. Increase The Orangutan Project's income to $20 million annually in order to fund and support these initiatives.

However, to achieve these large and audacious aims as well as carry on our existing projects, we need to expand our operations as an organisation. And also greatly increase our funding from all areas including donations, sponsorships, fund raising and grants. It is vital that we do this in the near future, because time is running out for the remaining orangutan populations in the wild. In our fight for our orange cousins, we are consistently pushing forward with our innovative and result-based projects into the future.

How We Do It....

What makes The Orangutan Project different from some other conservation organisations, and therefore more able to create lasting change through our projects, is our unique perspective and approach to the issues at hand. Because our work is not simply focussed upon the immediate problems which orangutans face, even though we do address these each day. Instead, we also work on the bigger picture to provide real solutions to the overall challenge of the orangutan's long term survival. In this way we are a solution based organisation.

I like to think of The Orangutan Project as being like a holistic doctor, who goes straight to the heart of his/her patient's problem by treating both the *cause of the illness* as well as the obvious *symptoms of the disease*. Because if we do not stop the cause of the orangutan's Critically Endangered status and only address the symptoms, we are merely offering a *band aid approach* which is ultimately destined to fail. And this is something which we do not intend to do.

Again, much like a doctor, we also appreciate that we need to apply different treatments or *medicines* to the different challenges we face. Our solution to this is to provide a number of distinct strategies and tactical responses depending upon the situation at hand. Each response designed to give us the best opportunity to support and save as many orangutans as possible.

Finally, in acute situations we also work with the idea of an emergency triage system. Triage is used by military doctors and also in hospital emergency wards. In these scenarios using the triage system, doctors will go in with the understanding that they have too many patients to deal with at the same time. Therefore they can't give optimum care to all of them at once and they have to separate patients into three different groups.

For example, with the triage approach, the doctor will say:

1. "You're too far gone. You're going to die whether I help you or not. Therefore we can make you comfortable for now however, you will inevitably die."
2. "You are OK and going to survive even without me helping you for the next day, so I'm not going to look at you right now either."
3. "Your injuries or issues are treatable, but you require my attention right now in order for you to survive. So individuals in this middle group can get my immediate help, because I can effectively help and save them now."

This doesn't mean the doctor lacks compassion for his or her patients, but this is the only way to relieve the most suffering and provide the most help with the resources available. Unfortunately, because we are not currently in the position to fully fund and address all orangutan conservation issues at once, we have to undertake a triage position in some unavoidable cases.

Focussing on What We Can Do...

However, as an holistic, hands-on, practical, big picture, organisation we ensure that we are being *proactive* for the long term, whilst being agile enough to handle as many as possible of the urgent and pressing problems requiring an immediate *reactive* approach. It is this unique perspective which has guided and governed our selection of projects and interventions for orangutans over the years. The result being that we work for orangutans on four specific fronts.

1. Rescue, Rehabilitation and Release
2. Securing and Protecting Natural Habitat
3. Education and Support of Local Communities
4. Changing the Game By Standing Up and Speaking Out

1. Rescue, Rehabilitation and Release...

In this area, we are supporting the vital work done in the field with high need cases. These include injured, ill and at risk wild orangutans as well as illegally held captives requiring rescue and rehabilitation. Ultimately, it is our aim to rehabilitate and re-release as many rescued orangutans back into their natural habitat. However where this is not possible due to injury, incapacitation or chronic illness, such cases are cared for in Quarantine Centres. To do this work The Orangutan Project collaborates with and supports existing conservation projects in addition to funding where needed, our own targeted on the ground programs.

The increased demand for orangutan rescue and rehabilitation is based upon a number of contributing factors.

Manmade impacts are predominantly due to the massive increase in industrial plantations, such as palm oil, pulp paper and rubber which have caused the greatest destruction to orangutan habitat across Sumatra and Borneo, plus the black market trade in orangutan infants. Added to this has been large scale deforestation due to unsustainable and illegal timber extraction and mining. So it is estimated that up to 80% of their natural forest habitat has already been destroyed.

Unfortunately, most wild orangutans are located outside of protected areas, leaving them even more vulnerable. If deforestation in Borneo and Sumatra continues to replace primary and degraded forests with unsustainable land uses such as oil palm plantations, then the incidence of human-orangutan conflict and orangutan starvation will increase, so it is unlikely that orangutans will survive in the long-term. It's a sad fact that direct orangutan killings continue to contribute to the decline in orangutan numbers.

Furthermore, human impacts have only been exacerbated by the natural social and cultural behaviours of the orangutans themselves. As the forests are cut down around them, female orangutans will generally stay put in their familiar, local territories. On the individual level, the female will typically sit in her tree with her infant waiting for things to improve even as the forest and trees begin to disappear. Ultimately she may hang on and hang on in an attempt to *wait the situation out* until there is just one tree remaining in an area. Sadly this means that a female orangutan and her baby will often be found in a lone tree as the loggers chop it down. The result being that the mother is slaughtered and the baby is taken for a pet or sold into the lucrative illegal animal trade.

On the other hand, the males are not necessarily attached to a territory and at the first signs of danger and hardship, will wander off to discover new feeding areas and new female orangutans to breed with… so they are usually long gone when the bulldozers move in and the people with the machetes arrive on the scene. However, the males may starve to death if they can't find enough food or may get caught raiding villages in search of something to eat and have to contend with violent attacks from upset locals.

As previously mentioned, the fact that female orangutans reproduce so slowly and care for their young so intensively, the average mating and birthing cycle for a Sumatran female is around nine years between each baby. Furthermore females have to reach around 14 to 15 years of age before they are ready to reproduce. This makes orangutans the most susceptible of all mammals to extinction. As a result of these factors, orangutan populations are estimated to have declined by well over 50% over the last 60 years and the threat of imminent extinction in the wild is very real.

It is the Orangutan Rescue Units and Rescue Centres, which are the frontline for orangutans in danger as they aim to provide a quick and skilled rescue response. From this point they will either relocate isolated or at risk orangutans back into the wild or take injured or ill . orangutans to rescue centres, if need be. Furthermore, rescue units assist authorities with law enforcement and confiscation raids on illegally held captive orangutans, as well as working to defuse and alleviate human-orangutan conflicts.

However, once orangutans are rescued, depending upon the extent of their injuries, age and general condition, they are relocated to Care Facilities, Rehabilitation Sanctuaries, Re-Release Sites or Quarantine Centres where they can be treated and cared for as needed. As you can appreciate, with such a high loss of orangutan forest habitat, these facilities are often under pressure and stress due to the constant demands on their services. Therefore The Orangutan Project funds a number of centres to support them in their critical, life-saving work.

Those orangutans able to be rehabilitated, may need to spend on average two to three years in Jungle Training Classes where they progressively learn the invaluable skills of sourcing and identifying foods, how to find water, tree climbing and navigation through the tree canopy. Social interactions with other orangutans, nest building, and general forest survival are also important skills they will need to survive in the wild. It was through the centre at Bukit Tigapuluh that both Tatok and the Perth Zoo orangutans Temara, Semaru and Nyaru were educated and trained before their release into the wild.

On the other hand, for the young orphaned orangutans separated from their mothers at a very young age, we must literally start from scratch with their training and education. This is because they have missed out on all of the cultural learning which would have been naturally passed on to them via their mother's dedicated nurture and care. Firstly, they need to be hand raised by experienced onsite technicians until they reach an age where they can begin Junior Jungle Training classes, before progressing to further training. This of course, takes a considerable time longer to achieve. This is where our successful Orangutan Adoption program supports the long and intensive process of rearing young and infant orangutans through childhood to adolescence and ultimately, release.

Once rehabilitated and ready for release, these orangutans are re-introduced into protected forest sites where they are regularly observed and checked by teams of Jungle Guardians. These vital post-release monitoring teams are committed to helping bridge the gap for orangutans from captivity to freedom, and they keep a watchful eye on the released individuals until they become independent.

Sadly, in the cases where rescued orangutans are permanently incapacitated or suffering afflictions ranging from human hepatitis through to paralysis and blindness, these orangutans can never be released. This is for their own safety and to prevent the spread of disease amongst wild populations. They therefore face the prospect of spending the rest of their lives in captivity (potentially as long as 60 years or more) and are held in Quarantine Centres until a more acceptable solution can be found for them.

Perhaps the best way to illustrate some of the excellent results that we have been able to achieve within this area, as well as some of the harsh realities we face, I'll share with you the stories of Leuser and Gober… two rescued orangutans who found new hope.

A Difficult Journey…

Leuser's remarkable story started back in 2004, when he was still an adolescent orangutan. He had been rescued via a confiscation raid when it was discovered that he was being illegally held as a pet in

Aceh Province. At the time of his rescue, he was fit and well and was therefore quickly released into the wild in Bukit Tigapuluh National Park, a protected area funded by The Orangutan Project. This was where Leuser was able to live happily as a wild orangutan, until late 2006.

Unfortunately, when we heard about Leuser again, he had been found near a village approximately 40km from the National Park boundaries, in an unprotected area. This time Leuser was not in good shape because he had been shot 62 times by local villagers with an air rifle. Three of the rifle pellets lodged in his eyes, rendering him totally blind as a result.

Veterinary surgeons were able to remove 16 of the pellets from his body, but 46 had to be left behind as removing them would have jeopardized his life…so they will remain in his body until he dies. As a consequence of shooting Leuser, three local villagers were jailed, all receiving sentences in excess of three months. The Orangutan Project funded the prosecution of the legal case. Leuser was returned to the Batu Mbelin Quarantine Centre in November 2006 for long term care.

Our story jumps to late 2008, when an older wild female orangutan named Gober, had to be rescued by the Sumatran Orangutan Conservation Programme (SOCP). Sadly Gober was captured in an area of mixed rubber and oil palm gardens completely isolated from natural forests because it was surrounded by oil palm plantations. The problem was that Gober was routinely raiding villager's crops to find food because she was blind in both eyes as a result of cataracts. If she had not been captured at the time she would surely have been killed by the disgruntled villagers.

So it was that Gober was also taken to the Batu Mbelin Quarantine Centre. With both Gober and Leuser being blind, their prospects for release were negligible and the best that could be hoped for them was to house them in the centre awaiting better conditions in the future.

Even though Leuser seemed to adjust to his new circumstances relatively well, as a wild orangutan of over 40 years of age, Gober did not settle in comfortably. Therefore after much consideration, it was decided by the centre's management that Leuser and Gober would be able to mate. As it was hoped that a new baby would give Gober something to focus her attention upon and significantly improve her mental state.

Finally, in 2011, Gober gave birth to healthy twin babies, a boy named Ganteng and a girl named Ginting. This was a particularly remarkable event as twin orangutan births are rare, and made even more so due to the fact that both parents were blind. Fortunately, known to be an experienced mother, Gober happily took to her maternal role and devotedly cared for the pair. But, due to her blindness, it was still thought that Gober would never be able to live in the wild again. However things would continue to look up for her and her spritely twins. As the twins became a part of The Orangutan Project's Adoption Program and many of our supporters started following their journey to freedom.

Soon afterwards, a top eye surgeon offered to carry out cataract surgery on Gober in an attempt to restore her eyesight. So in 2012 the doctor and the SOCP vet team performed the operation and it was a complete success. This meant that Gober gradually regained her vision and over time her eyesight was restored to almost 100%. With this unexpected turn of events, discussions began about the prospect of one day re-releasing Gober, with her twins, back into the wild. But at that time the babies were considered too young for release, so plans were put in place for the future.

Ultimately, in early 2015, after some time at the training and re-introduction site in Jantho, Sumatra, Gober and her twins were considered ready for freedom. During the release, Gober and her daughter, Ginting, were able to navigate the trees and forest environment and moved off quickly into the jungle. However, little Ganteng, the young male, was hesitant and not as confident in the trees as his experienced mother and nimble sister, and was subsequently left behind. It seemed that the years confined to a cage had reduced Gober's fitness so she was struggling to cope with her own challenges as well as the demands of looking after her daughter. Therefore she was not able to retrieve her reluctant son. Luckily the SOCP release team was able to keep him safely back in the facility for further training and care, until he was ready to attempt release again.

I wish that I could say that Gober and Ginting both lived happily ever after... but sadly this was not the case. Even though they were initially thriving within their natural habitat, a few weeks later, when I was visiting the release site, little Ginting's lifeless body was discovered on the forest floor. A distraught Gober was found in a nearby tree. It appeared that Ginting had fallen from the tree canopy and had died in the fall. All of us were devastated at hearing the news of Ginting's death.

Tragic as Gober, Leuser and the twin's story is, I share it here with you to highlight two very important points:

Firstly, the extreme challenges which we face in the *response based* area of orangutan rescue, rehabilitation and re-introduction. Although we have achieved undoubted success with orangutan releases and this work is vital to ensure the survival of the Critically Endangered Sumatran and Bornean orangutans, this type of approach is only a short term fix, at best. The truth is that it alone cannot solve this difficult problem, because it does not necessarily address the cause. Which brings me to my second point.

Ultimately the only solution to the end the spectre of orangutan extinction is a proactive, preventative and big picture perspective which means that we must work to create an environment in which orangutans can and will survive for generations to come. (Remember that to my way of thinking, the best rehabilitation centre is an empty one which no longer has a use because all of the orangutans are living safely, wild and free in protected areas.) This is why the Orangutan Project also focusses its attention on three other critical fronts to ensure a future for our orange cousins and it is here that we have some promising outcomes for real change.

2. Securing and Protecting Natural Habitat

Without a doubt, the number one most important long term solution is to secure and protect the orangutan's habitat. To save the orangutan we've got to save the rainforest in which they live. To do this we focus upon the purchase or lease of large tracts of forest suitable for orangutan populations, the direct defense of this land from illegal loggers and poachers, conservation projects to repair and rejuvenate at risk natural environments and targeted campaigns to stop further loss of rainforest to palm oil production and other unsustainable forms of agriculture.

It is important to note here, as someone who used to work as a small population geneticist managing zoo populations, that zoo orangutan populations, like most mega fauna are unsustainable, so there is no 'back up' ark. I often say – "It may be difficult to save orangutans in the wild, however it is impossible in captivity."

Ironically, as we continue to fight for natural habitat conservation, we are often met with the short sighted arguments of wildlife versus people or the environment versus the economy. However both of these positions are false. The protection of the rainforest not only benefits orangutans, but all wildlife which live alongside them, as it is the most biodiverse ecosystem in the world. In addition to this, the rainforest also benefits indigenous communities, which rely on the rainforest as their home, and local villages and communities which rely on the ecosystem and the services that the rainforest supplies for sustainable agriculture.

Furthermore the conversion of rainforest to unsustainable forms of agriculture, such as palm oil and pulp paper, is only economically rewarding for an elite few and actually passes on the *true cost of production* to the powerless. This in turn heavily impacts indigenous peoples, local communities and reduces the possibility of a sustainable economy for Indonesia. Ultimately it has massive environmental effects for all future generations across the globe. So the real question becomes, *"Do we let a few people in positions of power and influence destroy the forests and personally benefit at the expense of the many?"* because this destruction is fueled by a few multinational companies and is where the majority of profits go. I hope not.

The inconvenient truth is that the destruction of rainforest and natural habitat causes more global warming than all the transport systems in the world combined. So the protection of orangutan habitat fundamentally benefits all future generations on the planet. Therefore instead of seeing the plight of the orangutan as an issue localised to pockets of Sumatra and Borneo, we can appreciate that the protection of them as a species is a global concern. In fact, it should be viewed as an imperative for our own survival as a species.

For example, a coalition of conservation groups including The Orangutan Project obtained the management rights for two forestry concession blocks adjacent to the Bukit Tigapuluh national park or 30 Hills Ecosystem. The coalition focuses upon restoring and conserving 38,000 hectares of tropical rainforest in the area.

Once secured, our role has been to protect this natural environment, so teams of trained, skilled locals have been formed into Wildlife Protection Units (WPU). These units are fully funded by The Orangutan Project and are responsible for patrolling the 30 Hills ecosystem to deter and stop all illegal activities including logging, poaching and encroachment.

In their work, the WPU have foiled many illegal loggers, removed snares set by poachers, detected illegal logging camps and destroyed contraband wood when found. Recently the WPU encountered nine groups of loggers who all originated from nearby villages. They also undertake wildlife surveys to support orangutan conservation for the future.

This is why in the area of securing and protecting habitat, The Orangutan Project supports and funds many projects and we also have large goals to continue this vital work into the future.

3. Education and Support of Local Communities

When it comes to sustainable conservation efforts, the truth is that *ignorance is definitely not bliss.* Without the continued support, awareness and understanding of both local communities and the consistent flow of funds from concerned, compassionate and committed world-wide donors, we could not maintain our projects. Therefore education at the grass roots level with local children, the environmental guardians and community leaders of the future, is imperative as is our ongoing awareness programs and orangutan conservation campaigns within Indonesia, Malaysia and around the globe.

As an example of this, The Orangutan Project has provided school supplies and activities for the local schools near the Sumatran orangutan release site in the 30 Hills ecosystem /Bukit Tigapuluh and nearby communities. Here we have delivered a range of items including crayons, pencils, textas, puzzles, hand puppets and books. These were taken to educate and inspire the children about conservation and provide activities which encouraged role playing and reading about the animals which lived in the Bukit Tigapuluh jungle. It is important that the children know we care about them and their village as well as protecting the precious 30 Hills ecosystem. It is also vital that the local communities are supportive and understand the importance of forest conservation for their future livelihoods and survival.

Working with the Orang Utan Republik in Indonesia, we also run a Mobile Education Unit in Sumatra. This team is focused on implementing sustainable agricultural demonstration plots in two local villages to serve as test beds for organic, sustainable agricultural techniques that enhance yields and reduce impacts on wildlife and the environment.

The value of this to conservation is two-fold:

1. To build trust with the local farmers who are in direct conflict with the wild orangutan populations that occasionally raid crops, thereby facilitating the co-creation of humane strategies with the farmers to alleviate the conflict.
2. To provide techniques that will improve both crop yields with organic fertilisers and integrated pest management, and reduce their reliance on chemical fertilisers and pesticides that are expensive and unhealthy. Additionally, our teams undertake several school visits and tree planting excursions.

In this area The Orangutan Project supports multiple, ongoing education programs and has also held training sessions with local farmers, helped fund and build botanical nurseries, provided training on seed germination and preparation, harvested and sold vegetables grown organically to local eco-lodges, hosted classroom visits, created community participation programs during Environment Day, conducted activities in the villages during Orangutan Caring Week, distributed education campaign materials and organized multiple tree-planting activities which led to the planting of 2,550 trees in 2015, alone.

4. Speaking Out, Standing Up and Protecting their Rights

The final area in which The Orangutan Project operates covers a diverse range of activities and projects, all with one aim in mind… to change the game for orangutans across the planet. These initiatives include speaking out, standing up and fighting for the rights of all orangutans both legally and on moral and ethical bases. Through this work we hope to change the minds, open hearts and engender compassion for the support of orangutan survival and to avert their certain extinction under the current critical circumstances.

As well as funding legal prosecutions against illegal logging, poaching, intentional harm inflicted on orangutans and defence of their rights as sentient beings, we also work to impact land use planning and environmental conservation at the highest level of political and business decision making. Our ongoing advocacy and protection campaigns serve as a firm reminder to the humans and corporations who continue to harm and slaughter orangutans and destroy their remaining habitat that they will need to face the consequences of their actions. We are also active in defending the rights of those orangutans still held captive and to putting an end to their illegal trade around the world.

In fact in one recent case two infant orangutan babies were returned to one of the Sumatran Rescue and Refuge Centres we support, after they were discovered hidden in a suitcase at Kuwait airport. These two defenceless beings had been taken from their mothers via the illegal pet trade and were on their way to a life in captivity in a private individual's zoo. During their perilous transport they had been put into a suitcase with two oxygen cylinders in an attempt to keep them alive in transit. Fortunately this cruel and heartless act was foiled by customs security at the airport. However this trade continues to exist to this day due to demand and ignorance. It is therefore also our job to dispel the ignorance and arrogance displayed in acts such as these, and to gain universal recognition for our remarkable orange cousins' human rights.

I think perhaps the following story best illustrates some of the fantastic breakthroughs we have been able to achieve within this all important area.

Sandra, a Captive Orangutan in Argentina...

In 2014 I was approached by the Argentinian Lawyers' Association for Animal Rights to act as an expert witness on a case involving a captive female orangutan named Sandra. Sandra was being held in a Buenos Aires Zoo. She appeared depressed, spent much of her time hiding from sight and preferred to sit in the snow rather than submit to the amorous attentions of a co-captive male orangutan named Max.

In short she was displaying all of the characteristics of a person whose mental health was being negatively impacted by her captivity.

Because of this, the association, had filed a writ of *habeas corpus* alleging unlawful imprisonment of Sandra in the zoo and I was asked to testify – via Skype – on her behalf. I, of course, jumped at the opportunity to speak out for a being who could not do so for herself, so I accepted their request.

During this land mark case I was able to argue that because Sandra, a shy 30-year-old orangutan, displayed the characteristics of someone who knew her own mind she was therefore *a person* in the legal sense of the word. More importantly, I reasoned, that she should be accorded her rights as one.

Once my time before the Argentinian court was complete, it was left to the judge to deliberate and present her ruling on the case.

I am thrilled to say that on October 21, 2014, Judge Elena Amanda Liberatori handed down a decision which recognised that

Sandra, a captive orangutan, had rights. Furthermore she ruled that the government of the City of Buenos Aires had to guarantee adequate habitat conditions and necessary activities to preserve Sandra's cognitive abilities.

To me this ground breaking decision demonstrated that we are moving towards a shift in the blindly accepted cultural norms within society and that hearts and minds are slowly changing in regards to the rights of all sentient beings.

CHAPTER 9
WHAT YOU CAN DO

"How wonderful it is that nobody need wait a single moment
before starting to improve the world."
Anne Frank

Over the years that I have been working for orangutans, speaking out and campaigning for their rights, educating around the world and raising funds to ensure their survival, I have been both humbled and touched by the level of concern and support for the orangutan's plight. Because of this ground-swell of encouragement and assistance from good hearted and compassionate people across the globe, The Orangutan Project now has local chapters in Australia, Canada, New Zealand and the USA, with new ones planned for the future.

In addition to this, I regularly have the opportunity to reach out and connect with like-minded individuals as I speak internationally to share the message and importance of our cause. With our greater reach, The Orangutan Project is able to provide input, advice and feedback to assist in critical political environmental planning and land use decision making. As well as impact some business initiatives and fund legal cases to make people and companies who damage habitat, accountable.

Furthermore, we have also seen many positive flow-on effects from our conservation projects in Sumatra and Borneo. Which means that through our work in saving orangutans, we have also helped to protect other critically endangered species. These include animals such as the Sumatran tiger, elephant and rhino. Therefore to co-operate and further accelerate our results in the field, we also work alongside sister conservation organisations such as the International Elephant Project and International Tiger Project and Wildlife Asia… all with the ultimate aim to protect and conserve critically endangered mega fauna in the region.

However, where ever I go and with whomever I connect, the one question I am invariably asked is, *"Leif, how can I help save the orangutans?"*

As you can imagine, my immediate response is usually, first and foremost, *"Take immediate action and donate funds to The Orangutan Project and continue to do so until we have ensured the survival of the orangutan species."*

I am sure that you won't be surprised by my straightforward answer. Because in our world, money is the currency for *getting things done* and without it, we could not do the essential work we do and achieve the results we achieve for all orangutans. As my uncle, now a business man in America, used to say to his customers at his automotive repair centre in Sydney, *"There's nothing wrong that money won't fix!"* Now, even though this answer appears simplistic, it is certainly true as a vital first step, because the figures speak for themselves. As greater funding from donations to The Orangutan Project translates to more projects supported and greater outcomes for orangutans. In fact when you do the maths, it's clear that we could more effectively and efficiently get our aims achieved and the problems solved if we all just did our part financially as a society.

In addition to donating money to The Orangutan Project to fund and support our projects, there is a number of key things which you can start doing today which will have an enormous positive impact moving forward. To me, these actions are cumulative, with each building upon the next to solve the challenges facing orangutans and secure their future. I call them *The Five Things You Can Do, Starting*

Today and some of them may surprise you.

The Five Things You Can Do, Starting Today...

1. Change the Way You Think
2. Change the Way You Act
3. Change the Way You Buy
4. Change the Way You Vote
5. Change the Way You Give

1. Change the Way You Think

It's time for a change in our thinking and our approach, not only with how we treat orangutans, but all living beings on the planet. We each deserve to live with the freedom, respect and dignity which a life away from suffering and harm affords us. As well as being able to access and use the basic needs for survival, such as food, clean drinking water, fresh air, shelter and a peaceful environment. The sad truth is that not only are wildlife and the environment being endangered or destroyed, but millions upon millions of humans currently lack even the bare necessities of existence and struggle to simply survive.

But it doesn't have to be this way and a change in thinking holds the key.

To me, the first step for us to change the inequalities and injustices which occur in our world is to open both our minds and our hearts by being compassionate to all beings. In fact if we could simply extend compassion to all, our world would shift overnight. However to get to this point requires a new way of perceiving, one which combines the awareness of intellect and the love and empathy of our hearts. Because one without the other renders us ineffective as humans.

On one hand, the pure, detached logic of the intellect alone can be a cutting, hard and cruel master which seeks only a black or white answer. Especially when the solution may lie somewhere in between the two, in the more subtle shades of grey. Furthermore, to approach life in this simplistic, right/wrong paradigm means that our thinking lacks the benefits of the discernment of the heart and the wisdom of human kindness: Much like the idea of *profit at all costs* which disregards the rights and welfare of other living beings and will sacrifice these to achieve its targets.

On the other hand, to live and act solely from emotion exposes us to the danger of being governed by an ever changing array of unpredictable and irrational emotions and the corresponding attachments which occur when feelings alone, rule. As emotions are such unreliable states of being which can shift and change in an instant, yet cause so much devastation if acted upon without thought: Think of the husband who finds his wife in bed with another man, and who instinctively wants to kill this competitor for his wife's affections.

Therefore to be guided by either in isolation means that we are less able to appreciate the bigger picture, make informed choices and to ultimately act for the greater good of all. Much like the two wings of the bird, our task is to combine heartfelt empathy and love on the one side and then intelligently apply the clarity of mind and reason on the other, to the situation at hand. In this way we can all begin to act intelligently with compassion. When head and heart are aligned and love and compassion are at the centre of our choices, we are able to grasp the bigger vision, the greater purpose at play. In addition to this, we are no longer polarised or disturbed by the vagaries of emotions so the mind is more at peace and capable of seeing the whole solution not just the challenge in front of us.

This is what I call, *loving peace* which is a state of being where we are able to see *the good in the evil and the evil in the good*. With it there is balance of vision, a holistic way of seeing and greater meaning to life. Perhaps most importantly, we naturally move from being selfish or self-centred to being more selfless and life-centred. This is a shift which we all need to make in our thinking.

I have found that when my life is focussed upon the bigger purpose, the mission and the vision of The Orangutan Project I live a *larger life* and therefore do more for the cause. So the day to day, smaller things don't tend to bother me as much anymore, as they have become such a miniscule part of my world…much like a mosquito buzzing around me when I'm in the jungle, it is not a major upset nor a distraction to my day.

By taking up this *larger life* I have found I have been able to create an existence which has greater meaning for me on so many levels. Life is clearer, simpler and more peaceful and there is an inner freedom of being. Not only does it allow me to be free from the smaller issues of day to day life, it also makes me happier in the long run. As I can more clearly focus at the task at hand, see the difference our work is making, and the side effect of this is that I experience greater happiness.

The Meaning of Life…

The impact of this new way of thinking was demonstrated to me quite unexpectedly when I faced my mortality in a rain forest swamp.

From memory it was perhaps around 2004 and I had arranged to go into the rainforest for a few hours with two fellow conservationists and a local guide. Our task was to survey a particularly remote, dense patch of low lying swamp lands in Borneo. To understand the conditions in the area we were working, I'll just say that they were challenging and included facing dense jungle undergrowth, mosquitoes and other biting insects, swampy muddy leech infested waters and high temperatures with the correspondingly high levels of humidity. So prepared for the work ahead, we were dropped off into the area by boat, which was to collect us from a meeting point downstream at an agreed time later on in the day. Off we went and proceeded to wade through the local swamp as we surveyed the habitat.

As the hours wore on we found ourselves wading through muddy tepid swamp water which was by this stage, up to our waists. It was hot and it was hard going as we had thick, heavy rubber gumboots on which were now filled with water. This meant that with each step it felt as if we were having to lift many kilos at a time with our legs. Combined with this, one of my colleagues, developed heat stroke and began vomiting and retching uncontrollably as the afternoon progressed. Even worse still, our guide informed us that he had lost his bearings, was affected by malaria and we were now hopelessly lost within the swamp system.

As we had only prepared to be out for a few hours, we had no food supplies, little water and no camping equipment. With our friend being sick and needing to keep his fluids up, we were soon out of water. Shortly after this, we all began to feel ill as the harshness of the conditions caught up with us and heat exhaustion set in. Refusing to give up hope of finding our meeting place and our colleagues in the boat, we continued the increasingly difficult trudge through the swamp.

It was during this seemingly interminable trek that I contemplated the thought of dying here in a rainforest swamp in Borneo. By now I was physically exhausted, in pain and struggling with mental fatigue and, to me, it was becoming a real possibility that we wouldn't be getting out of there alive. It was growing late in the afternoon and all I could think about was finding a large tree to go and sit down under so I could be free of this struggle and just drift off peacefully to the release of death.

What surprised me though was that the thought of death, of leaving this life, did not concern me greatly. In fact, I found that if I stayed in the moment and focussed solely on what was occurring, I was strangely at peace. There was no sadness, no fear and no emotional pain in that moment. However, if I let my mind wander to the past and of those I loved, I suffered. Similarly, if I allowed my mind to focus on the future, what I would miss and my imminent death, I once again suffered. However, in the moment I felt a sense of love and calm. I was happy and would leave this life with no regrets. It was a surreal experience.

Having reached this inner state of letting go and being detached from the outcome, I struggled slowly onwards with the others with a peaceful heart and a quiet mind. Then suddenly, we heard calls in the distance. It was our friends in the boat. They had found us! We mustered what strength we could to call back to them and, with great difficulty, followed the sounds of their calls through the swamp and out to a larger waterway.

Needing help to get into the boat, due to our extreme exhaustion, we pretty much collapsed onto the bottom of the vessel. Remaining there to recover as our friends guided the boat slowly along the waterways back to camp. Internally I was happy to be alive, was but also intrigued by my own response to the situation. I had been able to observe within myself a way of thinking which was free of attachment and yet was very present in the moment and I had experienced a sense of compassionate love for all of life. It was something which I carried with me from this point forward.

2. Change the Way You Act

As it is said...*with greater knowledge comes greater responsibility.* So what is our responsibility as humans? Humans have responsibility because we have this knowledge. To become aware and yet take no action is to be worse off than those who are still ignorant of the facts. Therefore when we gain new insight or learn about a challenging situation and understand that it is vital to act in order to change the situation, we must act and act now. For to remain in inertia and to do nothing is to condone the issue by default.

Furthermore, there is a specific term which explains what happens when we learn some new facts or information, yet refuse to shift our view point and our actions based upon the newly comprehended truth. It's called *Cognitive Dissonance* and is a form of insanity where we choose to dismiss new knowledge because it doesn't fit into our existing world view. The result is that the offending information is blocked or rejected by our reptilian brain (or brain stem and cerebellum) which acts as the gate keeper to the mind. Therefore we refuse to see the truth which is right in front of us and remain inactive as a result. However, the problem is that it's not the new idea, data or information which is defective. Instead it is our rigid and tightly held opinions, beliefs and ways of seeing the world which are at fault.

As the renowned conservationist and animal rights campaigner, Peter Singer, points out: sanity = awareness, insanity = ignorance.

So the question becomes, who or what do we want *running the show* in our lives, our insanity or our awareness? The answer has to be our awareness which means that we must act upon it.

For me, both personally and professionally Peter Singer was one of the sanest men I have ever met. It was he to whom I turned when I was struggling with reconciling my role at the zoo whilst my conscience no longer supported the practice of holding orangutans in captivity. I asked Peter his advice and he said to me, *"Leif, remain at the zoo for as long as you can do good and make a difference and leave when you can no longer do so."*

And that is what I did.

In terms of what we can all do now to change the tide for the orangutans, I recommend taking the following steps:

- ✓ Take purposeful action today and join The Orangutan Project to ensure the positive steps we have already taken, continue into a lasting legacy for the future for all orangutans.

- ✓ Visit our website at www.orangutan.org.au and become a donor and a supporter today.

- ✓ Offer your services as a Volunteer with The Orangutan Project and get to meet like-minded people with a common mission and cause whilst working to raise funds and awareness for the orangutans.

- ✓ Join us on social media by following our facebook page and posts. Like, share and join the conversations, because everyone makes a difference and your voice counts.

- ✓ Speak up and communicate with others and if any of the stories and insights you've gained from this book have inspired you, share your thoughts with friends and family. Your words have power and sharing ideas on how we can all save the orangutans can inspire and educate others.

- ✓ Recommend this book if you've enjoyed it or buy some for gifts and spread the story of our orangutan friends and the actions which will save them from extinction, across the globe.

- ✓ Be proactive; change the way you eat by becoming a vegan, a vegetarian or at least consider greatly reducing your meat and dairy intake and educate yourself why this is the best way to go. Because the truth is that, livestock and dairy agriculture and the intensive meat production industry are the number one biggest cause of global warming and animal suffering on the planet. (I will discuss this in further detail in Chapter 12)

✓ Grow your own fresh produce where possible using organic, bio dynamic and environmentally friendly fertilisers and composts.

The key is to get into action and do something today, because there will never be a more perfect time than the present moment and the orangutans need our help now.

3. Change the Way You Buy

The way that you spend your money acts as a silent, but powerful vote of approval. The combined consumer demand for a product or service or lack of demand for that same product or service will ultimately determine whether is it produced or made available, or not. This is because a company will generally not continue to create a product or offer a service which no one buys and for which there is no market. As they are in business to make a profit and stock which doesn't sell causes them to lose, not make money. Therefore, as consumers, we all have enormous buying power when it comes to having a direct impact on which items make it onto our supermarket shelves and out into the market in general…it's just that we don't necessarily exercise this power in an organised and targeted way.

However, we can make a difference in this area if we become aware of the ingredients or components contained in the products we buy, how they are manufactured, how they are trialled, tested and researched, where they are made and how the workers who make them are treated…and then vote with our purchases by buying according to the following:

- ✓ The most obvious product to avoid is cheap and readily available palm oil and any products containing unsustainable palm oil, but it's important to note that, in and of itself, avoiding palm oil is not the solution which will save the orangutans. (I'll discuss the real cost of palm oil in chapter 11) As well as illegally logged rain forest woods from Indonesia and Malaysia.

- ✓ Support and use solar, wind and renewable power sources.

- ✓ Buy natural, fresh, organic and unprocessed produce and only purchase and support products made from sustainable, humane and renewable resources wherever possible.

- ✓ Stop buying and eating meat and all products containing animal by-products in their ingredients.

- ✓ Refuse to purchase any health products, natural remedies, personal care products, make up or skin care which contain animal by-products or are produced as a result of animal testing or cruelty.

- ✓ Stop buying clothing manufactured by companies or brands recognised for using sweat shop, low paid or child labour.

- ✓ Ensure that your cleaning products are environmentally friendly and low impact where possible.

✓ Avoid or limit your use of highly toxic or chemically based items in your home and business.

4. Change the Way You Vote

If you are a citizen of a *democracy*, I think that we can become relatively blasé and complacent about our rights and the power we wield when we vote for a political representative. Unfortunately, within Australia and most western democracies, we are confronted with a predominantly two party political system, where there is little real difference between the aims and behaviours of the two main parties. However, in recent years there has been a proliferation of smaller parties and some outspoken independents entering the field.

This is where we can make a difference with the way in which we vote, by voting for representatives who support humane, people based values and environmental conservation. To do this we need to move our political support away from ruling elitist parties and neo colonialist influences to those who champion a fairer opportunity for all, as well as forward-thinking environmental policies to protect the rights of all living beings and the natural habitat in which they live. So we can create the place which R. Buckminster Fuller describes as the Earth of the future:

"A world which works for everyone, with no one left behind."

To achieve this, I see that we need to secure true democracy which involves:

✓ Free and fair press and mixed media ownership.

✓ Have publicly funded elections only, where competing business and/or union interests are not favoured and protected over the majority of citizens. Our investment in this will be returned to our society many times over.

✓ A wider range of choice in the political arena with new parties entering the field which are free of the old, restrictive two party system.

✓ Ensure that companies, organisations and individuals which impact the environment are made to pay for the true cost of production, rather than allowing them to pass these costs onto the local communities and the future generations to come.

✓ Begin to elect leaders and political parties which work for the greater good of the community, the country and the planet as a whole.

✓ Put policies and initiatives into place which have forward thinking timelines of 50 to 100 years into the future, rather than the short term two to three year plans based around an election cycle.

For me as an observer of the 2016 US elections there was a real chance for change with the wide support for the candidate Bernie Sanders, it has been incredible to watch as the race has come down to a *choice* between Hilary Clinton and Donald Trump. As how can it be called democracy when the only way to vote is for the lesser evil of the two?

5. Change the Way You Give

As I've already mentioned, the number one most impacting action you can take for the orangutans, is to get on-board and make a regular donation to The Orangutan Project. From there we can make your valued funds go to work to ensure their survival on your behalf. Many people think that they have to commit a large amount of their income each month to be able to make any real difference for the cause. However, I can assure you that for as little as $20.00 per month you could be supporting the care and development of one of the young orphaned orangutans who are part of our *Adoption Program*. So don't think that you have to donate a large lump sum all at once – although these will always be appreciated- but understand that it is the regular, ongoing donations which ultimately keep our vital work for the orangutans funded over the long term.

Even if you start small, you can always increase your donation level at a later date, if you choose. The key here is to simply start and to take action now by joining the movement to save the orangutan. Because the truth is, most of The Orangutan Project's funding comes from small regular *community grass roots donations* and every dollar raised is important. Because it's the ongoing donations over a large fundraising base which provides the most stable form of income for The Orangutan Project, as conservation is always about the long-term. And, yes, we hope that one day there will be a utopian society where the government and its processes will protect habitat and ecosystems, but at the moment that stable form of income provides the most effective form of conservation.

It's not the intensity of your support but the broadness and perspective of your support which makes the difference

There is a wide variety of options when it comes to making your contribution to support the orangutans. This means you can choose to donate in any of these ways:

✓ Set up an automatic donation on a regular monthly basis at a level which is comfortable to you, no amount is considered too small.

✓ Support specific appeals such as securing areas of habitat, funding Rescue Centres, Release Programs or Wildlife Protection Units, etc.

✓ Be part of our Orangutan Adoption program by sponsoring an orphaned orangutan in need of care.

✓ Join us on one of our exciting Orangutan Adventure Tours for a unique first-hand experience of seeing the orangutans and their forest home.

✓ Opt to become one of our Business Partners and offer your team the opportunity to contribute via their workplace.

✓ Or perhaps consider leaving a lasting legacy by including The Orangutan Project in an End of Life Bequest in your Will.

The choice is up to you and the orangutans will directly benefit from your contribution, as I know that we can save the orangutans from extinction. What's more, the great news is that you won't be doing this alone and if we all work together to contribute our own small bit and each play our part, then we can make a real and lasting difference. So join us and help our orangutan friends stay safe and live free, because a small group of committed individuals can change the world.

SECTION 4

THE BIGGER GAME AT PLAY AND PHILOSOPHICAL PERSPECTIVES

*"What humans do over the next 50 years will determine
the fate of all life on the planet."*
Sir David Attenborough, Broadcaster & Naturalist

CHAPTER 10
A SHIFT IN THE WAY WE SEE

"Humankind has not woven the web of life.
We are but one thread within it.
Whatever we do to the web, we do to ourselves.
All things are bound together. All things connect."
Chief Seattle, 1854

Even though I am a zoologist, I am also a philosopher at heart. This is because I am inspired by the way the age old questions about life, and humanity's place within it, are still as relevant today as they were thousands of years ago. However, to me no philosophical perspective or way of viewing existence is worthwhile or complete unless it manifests as action in the world. By this I mean that the greater insight or knowledge can be used to gain deeper understanding, solve real issues and create new and improved outcomes for all. Therefore I have always looked to the experiences and events of life for the lessons on how to best navigate the highs and the lows, the successes and the challenges along the way. Because I have learned that life is a good, but cruel teacher and it is often through my greatest hardships that I have found the most significant truths.

This has certainly been demonstrated throughout my personal and professional journey with my much loved friends, the orangutans. As it has been via my personal quest to save them that I have come to understand the truth of the key philosophical insights which I will cover in this final section of the book. The reason I wish to share them with you is not that I believe I have anything unique to offer, but to share my ways of perceiving the world and being within it. These have greatly assisted me to do the work I do and to achieve the results that we have attained through The Orangutan Project…and still remain relatively happy and sane in the process. I also hope that you can relate to these ideas and know that you are not alone.

Therefore in the closing sections of this book, I will focus upon a key idea and then apply it to some of the issues which I have had to come to terms with and resolve, both within my own psyche and in the way I perceive the world at large. Some of these ideas may surprise you and some of their applications may challenge you. However, I encourage you to keep an open heart and mind whilst you consider them. At the very best, they may just change the way you see the world and act within it…or at the least, you will be aware of alternative approaches to some of life's pressing questions.

Oneness of All Life…

One of the foundational philosophical perspectives which I embrace and share with others is the concept of the *Oneness of All Life*. It is neither a new idea nor an uncommon one, as many of the world's greatest philosophers and thinkers, from Thales of Greece to Hildegard of Bingen, from Emerson, Blake and Whitman to Bohme, Plank, Einstein and even Jung spoke of the unity and interconnectedness of existence. In addition to this, many ancient and modern indigenous cultures hold this tenet at their core, and in recent years, research by quantum physicists into the behaviour of sub atomic particles within the quantum field points to this same idea of oneness. The truth is that from the microscopic through to the macroscopic perspective, we are all part of this oneness. In addition, scientific experiments, such as those now showing that matter is not fixed until observed, this oneness is not inert but is sentient and linked to our conscious experiences. For example, at the quantum level, we know that everything within the universe is comprised of matter or energy. Matter is manifest energy and both are ultimately *vibrations* in the single field of existence through which the manifest universe arises.

In living beings, matter in the form of atoms of constituent elements make up the cells of the body, which form into specialised internal systems resulting in a living organism. As living organisms we live on a planet comprised of a range of interconnected eco systems which are based upon the unique climatic conditions, vegetation, geology, geography and topography of the location.

As a whole, our planet is governed by the natural laws of physics which seem to be consistent across our solar system, galaxy, the universe, as we know it, and perhaps even those we don't yet know. So therefore, all life on planet Earth shares a part in the oneness of existence. And at our core we are much more connected than disconnected, more alike than different, because we are all literally made of the same *stuff of the universe*.

Running Free with Temara...

I have been asked, if it is possible for a human to experience oneness with an orangutan? And my answer is yes, as I clearly remember sharing one such moment with Temara, after her release, which will forever remind me of this reality.

In 2006 whilst Kylie and I had taken, Temara, the zoo born orangutan, on her history making return to the wild, I was spending some time monitoring her after her release into the rainforest. At the time, Temara was high up in the tree canopy, exploring her new surroundings and generally making herself at home. Meanwhile Kylie and I were positioned underneath her tree in order to observe her movements. We were relieved and happy and everything seemed to be going to plan.

However, all of a sudden we saw Temara clambering down the tree trunk at record speed with a huge, angry swarm of jungle bees in hot pursuit. She must have unknowingly disturbed a bee hive high up in the canopy and now they were after her. In a moment Temara was down on the ground with us and in that same instant we were all set upon by the aggressive stinging bees. (Interestingly, bees and falling wood are the biggest killers in the rainforest, not tigers and bears as most people expect.) Shocked and unaccustomed to this targeted attack by the bees, Temara instinctively set off running along the forest track with myself, Kylie and the bees following.

Now in that moment, as we raced through the forest being stung by bees, there were a few things running through my mind. Firstly, our job was to make sure that Temara stayed up in the trees and spent as little time on the ground as possible, otherwise she could end up as lunch for a tiger. Secondly, she was covering a huge amount of ground in a short space of time due to her efforts to escape the bees and although I was able to keep up with her, unfortunately Kylie had been left behind in the rush. So it was very important that I stayed with her and did not lose sight of our precious orange friend. Thirdly, the incredible nature of our situation dawned on me. Here I was running through the jungle in Sumatra with a once captive orangutan, trying to outrun a very determined swarm of bees… it was one of those *truth is stranger than fiction* instances.

Finally we seemed to have left the bees behind us and, in exhaustion, both Temara and I slumped down against the trunk of a large tree so we could catch our breath. Sitting shoulder to shoulder with our backs to the tree, gasping for air and not without a number of bee stings each, Temara and I must have looked a sight. As we both began to regain our composure I turned my head to look at her and Temara did the same. We looked into each other's eyes in acknowledgement of our close shave, but what struck me was that we were no longer playing our roles as a human conservationist and a rehabilitated captive orangutan. Instead we were simply two beings who had just shared an amazing encounter together in the forest and everything else had slipped away...we were equals and were at one.

After this brief recognition between us, we both stood up and I said to Temara in Indonesian, "*Naik, naik.*" Which literally means *climb, climb* and was the learned instruction for her to go back up into the tree canopy, where she would be safe from hungry predators. Temara obliged by carefully making her way up the tree trunk and we reassumed our respective roles.

So for me the truth of oneness is all around us and is available to experience in the moment if we are willing to drop our barriers to it.

The Great Lie of Separation...

However, for some reason, there is a misconception across much of humanity. One which consistently promotes the idea of separation and difference, which serves to perpetuate a '*them and us*' mentality. Usually based upon the seeds of fear, hate, ignorance, greed and competition, the world in which we live is incessantly divided along arbitrary and competing lines amongst people and other living beings.

For example, we are divided by allegiances to our: family / community / state / country / continent / region / nationality / race / religion / culture / gender/sexual preference / beliefs / diet / political ideals and even our sporting teams.

In addition to this we are compared and compartmentalised as humans based upon our wealth / age / health / intelligence / physical ability / social status / the clothes we wear and our material possessions.

To further compound the issue are the false perceptions of competing interests such as the *individual versus society, environment versus the economy* and *wildlife versus people.* Furthermore there is the random and irrational segregation of differing forms of life into those we value and treat with esteem and those we treat with abuse and cruelty. Yet each of these distinctions and divisions is purely of our own subjective invention, based upon the misconception of separation. Not only do they not serve us as a species, they actually reduce the likelihood of our survival.

In reality, as beings living on Earth, we all share this planet as our home. Therefore the actions and behaviours of one group of beings correspondingly impacts upon the lives of all other beings on the planet. So, it is much more useful to view any issue or challenge from the bigger perspective of oneness of all life, instead of from our own individual, ego based standpoint. Especially if we aim to come up with viable long term solutions which work for all. Interestingly, it is known that astronauts, of all nationalities and creeds, who are fortunate enough to travel into space and view our beautiful blue green planet from this distant perspective, commonly report experiencing life changing shifts in the way they see the world. In fact, from space, our man-made boundaries and self-imposed divisions appear not only inconsequential, but simply absurd.

Our task becomes to shift our perspective to encompass the oneness of all life and to see the bigger picture on planet Earth. Because it is time to come out of our old tribal mentality and exercise an inclusive more humane strategy rather than the old paradigm of exclusion and conflict. With this in mind, we need to remove these arbitrary barriers and collapse the beliefs and prejudices which keep the perception of separateness in place. To do so it is useful to understand the distinction between *prejudice and pre judgement.*

In the case of pre judgement, I see this as a survival mechanism which is in our nature. With this skill, even though we may have made a pre judgement, we can always re-choose at any point within an encounter. Especially once we receive more information, understanding and insight to help us make a better judgement. This is because we are still open minded and open hearted in the moment and the element of love is present.

However, where there is prejudice in place it keeps us stuck in our rigid pre-defined position. This serves to keep us blind to the truth, which is actually right in front of us, because we cannot see past our own fixed perspective. Ultimately, it is ingrained prejudice and cultural falsehoods which end up killing us and have us killing other beings, because the elements of fear, hate, ignorance and arrogance are present within these perspectives.

Puan's Choices Based on Her Past...

Even orangutans can be prejudiced and I have personally witnessed orangutans demonstrate both pre judgement and prejudice.

As mentioned, Puan was a wild born female orangutan who had witnessed the murder of her mother. She was sent to Perth Zoo many years ago after being held in Johor Zoo, Malaysia. Unbeknown to the orangutan keepers in Perth, Puan must have also been poorly treated by her previous keepers, because she had developed an enduring prejudice towards any human who looked like her prior captors. This meant anyone of Asian extraction. In fact, Puan wasn't too fussed with humans in general, however if people of Asian descent were present, she would often become agitated and aggressive and would not tolerate their presence.

Unfortunately it was hard for Puan to shift her limited, racially based viewpoint. Therefore she missed out upon the potential benefits of forming relationships with a large group of people because she was not able to overcome her prejudice, even if presented with new people or events. Thus Puan remained blind to the possibility that the decisions she had made about her past experiences may not have been true in all cases.

On the other hand, Puan's daughter, Puteri, the first orangutan to be born in Perth Zoo in 1970, did not demonstrate the same prejudice towards Asian people. As an open minded individual, Puteri, was able to make more effective choices as she came to know and, ultimately, like humans. She grew more and more comfortable with us during the contact sessions she shared with myself and other team members. In fact, as mentioned earlier, Puteri grew to be an exceptionally affectionate orangutan who loved nothing more than sharing hugs during our interactions within her enclosure. So she did not let her pre judgement limit her experience of the world, as her judgement remained fluid and open to changes in understanding and knowledge.

Therefore because Puteri was exercising pre judgement, she was able to shift her perspective based upon new information and experiences. Whilst Puan continued to remain stuck in her preconceived prejudices. So the distinction between the two states of pre judgement and prejudice, ultimately centres on openness to love and the willingness to experience it. Furthermore, in order to perceive oneness with all life, we need to practice love for others, instead of making them wrong and building barriers between each other. It is important to note that Puteri is, and remains to this day, a far happier being than Puan. Interestingly, despite her unique disposition, Puan recently celebrated her 60th birthday at Perth Zoo and was recognised by the Guinness Book of World Records for becoming the oldest Sumatran orangutan held in captivity.

The truth is that we live in a sea of love and it is our ego, individual identity and prejudices which cloud this understanding and keep us blind to the special moments of connection with the oneness. It is only by letting go of our ego or individual stand point and embracing the awareness of love, that we can open the window to our true essence, and the true essence of all life, which is oneness.

So the question is, *"How does the oneness of all life apply in real life circumstances?"*

Applying Oneness within Conservation...

Within my field of work in conservation and animal welfare, I have also witnessed many prejudices and barriers arise between humans and experienced their damaging impacts. However surprisingly, I have found that some of the most angry, aggressive and prejudiced individuals were also those who seemingly belonged to what I perceived as *my side or the good side,* the side of conservation and animal rights. As over time, these people became stereotypical examples of the angry, bitter and misunderstood environmentalist. Instead of being rebels without a cause, they became rebels who had a cause but who had gotten lost somewhere along the way.

When Fighting Monsters...

For example, I remember a conservation meeting where I was part of a group of conservationists who were to meet with some representatives from companies with interests in destructive industries such as palm oil and logging. So, as you'd appreciate, to some conservationists we were literally sitting down with *the enemy* as the interests of these companies appeared to be at opposite ends of the scale to our own. However, we were there to work together with the different stakeholders to achieve our aim of securing the protection and conservation of rainforest habitat into the future.

As the discussion got underway and the differing perspectives were presented, I could see that some of the members of *my side* were beginning to get quite heated and defensive in their responses and attitudes to the other people at the table. Furthermore, over the course of the meeting I witnessed some of the conservationists descend into being rude and aggressive individuals. In fact, they were by far the worst behaved and the least respectful people in the room. Instead of promoting our cause, they were so entrenched in speaking their minds and *being right* that they only made our task all the more difficult to achieve. The task which would have helped save and protect not only orangutans and their native habitat, but many of the other mega fauna, such as elephants, tigers and rhinos in the area. However, their hate and resentment rendered them unable to hold the bigger picture in mind and work for the best outcome possible for their cause. Ultimately, a few of my colleagues were the ones who had become monsters, monsters of their own making. As the old saying goes, "*Before fighting monsters, be careful not to become one yourself.*"

When I first encountered this type of behaviour amongst conservationists, it puzzled me. This was also the case when I observed the internal destruction within my mentor Reg Gates when he could no longer cope with the difficult situations which confronted him at the zoo. In addition to this, I too found that I had to be mindful and stop myself from becoming a bitter, angry and frustrated individual as a result of the injustices occurring for orangutans. It was here that I began to see a pattern and came to appreciate what could happen within me and within good hearted and well-meaning individuals… many of whom were my friends and colleagues.

Don't Become an Environmental Martyr…

I came to identify this phenomenon as Environmental Martyrdom, where good people lose their way and literally martyr themselves for their particular environmental, conservation or animal welfare cause. However, I also knew that it didn't have to be this way, so I decided to look for an answer, but to start with I wanted to understand why it happened.

Firstly I saw that there was a selfish hate cycle, which caused a seething self-justified and rigid right/wrong mindset. This way of seeing perpetuated itself by focussing only upon what it was *fighting against,* instead of what it *stood for* in the bigger picture. Once caught in this this cycle, I saw selfless, life-centred people become embittered and self-centred. Much like a piece of fruit beginning to rot from the inside out, I witnessed many kind, well intentioned people turn bad. These were people who called themselves animal-lovers, environmentalists and conservationists, yet they turned from being positive, good hearted people into angry and vicious individuals. So by the end of the process, they had hate in their hearts and minds and were even capable of being violent in the name of their cause.

I also learned that environmental martyrs essentially become fanatics and all fanatics use a cause to justify their bad behaviour. (Think of terrorists, religious fundamentalists and extremists) More importantly, by acting as such, in the end they help no one and can actually damage the very cause for which they fight. With fanatics it becomes an ego based way of being and they start fighting others in an attempt to control and coerce them to do their bidding. The problem is that most people and living beings do not respond well to this type of approach, therefore their actions create opposition, which in turn, makes them even more frustrated. Ultimately they can't see past their position due to their ego, and the fight becomes all about them. Strangely they still want others to think that they are *good people,* however, what happens is that they mentally transfer their bad behaviour onto others and actually become worse than those they fight.

Unfortunately, this occurs when good hearted people, people like you and I, get caught up in the highly emotional nature of the area of conservation and animal welfare. Without doubt, it is a difficult field especially when we see animals and people suffer, habitat destroyed and short term greed and ignorance govern decisions about the environment. However, nowhere is it more important to be aware and in control of emotions, reactions and resulting prejudices as these can so easily form within our hearts and minds. The key is to not let these rule, but to combine the reason and logic of the mind plus the compassion and love of the heart, whilst keeping the bigger picture of oneness within. With this approach, it is possible to remain effective and still make a difference.

However, without the bigger perspective of oneness being applied to issues of conservation, there are only two ways in which it can go for an emotionally charged individual.

1. The emotional charge pushes outward to attack and drives you to destroy others.

   So you lash out and belittle others and their opinions or you express explosive anger. And if you hurt others in the process, you justify it by telling yourself that you're doing it for the *cause* or for the animals, and thereby let yourself off the hook for your poor behaviour. (Like my colleagues in the conservation meeting).

2. The emotional charge turns inwards upon yourself and you struggle to cope at the inner level. So you turn this frustration, anger and hate upon your own inability to make a difference and you destroy yourself because you cannot handle the pain of it all. Therefore you implode under the weight of your inner turmoil and feelings of impotence in the face of the constant struggle of your right position against their perceived wrongs. (Like Reg when he could no longer cope at the zoo.)

For people in our field and those who support us, the choice must be to focus on love not loss, on connecting with people and bringing them along *with us* to make a change which will be for the common good. However, this is not possible if we lose our equilibrium and become emotionally charged with anger, hate, fear and the arrogance which comes from a perspective of *I am right and you are wrong*. The key here is to resist the desire to see ourselves as superior and to always *act because we care*, not in order to make others wrong. Using the concept of oneness, we can remove the barriers of separation and otherness and reframe the discussion to a wider perspective which is inclusive not exclusive, and not based upon the, *I'm right and you're wrong* paradigm. By coming from the perspective of compassion and love for all beings, and working with people for change, in the spirit of co-operation not confrontation, we create a greater common cause.

To do this, I had to lift myself out of the narrow perspective of the choice between right and wrong, and this took a total paradigm shift in my way of seeing things. I had to move my perspective to seeing the whole of the picture, as from above the issues, instead of viewing events from within them. So I moved from anger and fear, black and white, from attachment and hate, right and wrong to love and oneness.

Remember, in the very beginning of this book I shared the stories of Perth, the rescued, wild born orangutan in Sumatra and Chantek, the sign language using, captive male in the USA. It was my experiences with them which ultimately precipitated my choice to found The Orangutan Project. Yet if I had not been able to see the bigger perspective and the possibility to create positive change for all orangutans, I would have never embarked upon this journey. It was through my appreciation of oneness and my belief that if we all worked together for a better solution for all, that we could save the orangutans from extinction. And it is this ethos which has helped The Orangutan Project develop and expand into the innovative and effective conservation organisation it is today.

"Love is the ultimate meaning of everything around us.
It is not a mere sentiment.
It is truth; it is the joy that is at the root of all creation."
Rabindranath Tagore

CHAPTER 11
THINKING DIFFERENTLY...

"An unexamined life is not worth living."
Socrates

One of my favourites amongst the ancient Greek philosophers, is Socrates, a great thinker who lived around two and a half thousand years ago. In particular, it was more than Socrates' specific beliefs and ideas on the universe which drew me to his work, because I came to appreciate his approach to logical discussion and debate. This approach became known as Critical Thinking or the Socratic Method and what I most admired about this method was that Socrates was the master of asking intelligent questions. Moreover he was able to formulate and pose questions of such simplicity and discernment that in order to answer them, the individual on the receiving end of his penetrating queries had to think clearly and definitively to provide an answer. So with my naturally enquiring mind, Socrates' philosophies on logical inquiry resonated with my understanding that:

The quality of my life and the results I achieved, were directly impacted by the quality of the questions I asked of myself and those around me.

Combined with my exposure to scientific enquiry in university, I began to more fully question my own assumptions about the realities of life as well as the assumptions of others within my personal and professional sphere. Importantly, I think with regard to my work for orangutans and within the field of conservation, this approach has made all the difference for me. When confronted with a prevailing mind set or mainstream belief system, I was able to ask questions which both challenged the accepted view, whilst at the same time, pushed for a better solution to the existing situation.

In many ways, I suppose that this may have made me seem like a rebel or a non-conformist to some, and this was definitely the case at the zoo. However, within the realm of orangutan conservation, I found that it gave The Orangutan Project as an organisation, an added dimension when dealing with the difficult issues which we faced. As it provided us with the balanced perspective I spoke about earlier in Chapter 9, where we had the *two wings of the bird* or the combination of the compassion of the heart and the clarity and reason of the mind, at our disposal. It may appear as a simplistic distinction, however, it's only by asking different questions that we are able to uncover and appreciate different answers.

The Socratic Method...

The process of the Socratic Method of thinking revolves around asking questions which challenge commonly held assumptions and generally accepted ways of seeing the world. By a process of elimination, the type of questions asked begin to reveal inconsistencies and underlying contradictions within the original precept. In doing so the idea, which is literally being put under the microscope of reason and logic, either develops into a more considered and truthful concept or, by virtue of its integrity, stands the test of intelligent questioning and is proven to be correct. So Socrates was able to develop a form of logical inquiry which became recognised as the fore-runner of our modern day scientific method.

Interestingly, Socrates was known to publicly state that he himself knew *nothing* and that he was an ignorant man. In fact, during his trial before the citizens of Athens he famously stated, *"I know that I know nothing."* However, what he was actually saying with these statements was that, he was aware of his ignorance. And, it was due to this awareness, that he was wiser than those who were ignorant, yet still considered themselves knowledgeable. This paradox of thinking allowed Socrates to maintain both his humility and his insight into his own fallibility...both exceptionally wise qualities to possess. [18]

The Socratic Thinking Process...

1. Identify a commonly accepted assumption or belief and formulate it as a statement. This becomes your original *truism*.

2. As part of the process, approach the *truism* as if it is false and seek out circumstances or perspectives from which it could be seen as untrue.

3. Where a contradiction, inconsistency or exception to the *truism* is found, it must therefore be false.

4. At this point, the original *truism* described by the statement, needs to be expanded and enhanced to take the inconsistency into account. Thereby creating the newly improved statement of truth.

5. If at any point the new statement/truism is found to be false or involve contradiction, the process is then started again. [19]

Even though the process is deceptively simple, Socrates always stayed loyal to the concept that, *"The product of thought, is superior to the product of intuition."* And to support his argument he used the example of the two products of truth derived from either thought or intuition as being like the statue of a great sculptor.

In the case of a truth produced by *intuition*, it was likened to a statue erected without the firm foundation of a stabilising base or plinth. In that, a strong wind or a sudden knock could cause it to fall over at any time.

However where a truth was firmly supported by *logic, intellect and reason* as well as the awareness of any counter arguments against it, the statue was held firmly in place by the strong and stabilizing forces these provided. [20]

Therefore by applying the Socratic Thinking Process as outlined, I'd like to put some of the common assumptions we encounter in our work to the test, both at the personal and the wider levels.

Palm Oil is a Cheap Product...

Truism: Everyone we speak to within the palm oil industry believes that palm oil is a good, cheap and readily available product. They "prove" their assumption by explaining that the reason palm oil is in so many of the products we buy these days, is because it's cheap. In fact it is so cheap, that manufacturers can afford to put it in everything. Therefore, from their perspective, palm oil is certainly a cheap product.

Question to Find Untruth: However, is this actually true? Because I put forward the proposition that palm oil is actually one of the most expensive products in the world today.

Evidence of Falsity: When people hear me say this, they may think that, "*Leif's gone a bit crazy here,*" but what I'm saying is, there are huge inconsistencies and contradictions within this argument.

For example, the rainforest provides extensive natural ecosystem services to protect against global warming and preserve water catchment, fisheries, non-forest products of the local communities and the food for indigenous people. These services therefore have an enormous monetary value. So, if the palm oil companies had to pay compensation or pay for the replacement of all of those ecosystem services which the rainforest has been providing and supporting before it was destroyed, to create palm oil plantations, they couldn't do it. In fact, their business case and financial plan wouldn't add up or produce any profit.

However, what the palm oil companies do is pass the true cost of converting the forest to palm oil onto the powerless, e.g. the orangutans and other endangered species, indigenous peoples, local communities, the long term Indonesian economy as a whole and global warming for future generations. In this way, there is a cost, but this cost is kept invisible by the palm oil companies because it never appears on their profit and loss statements. However, morally companies cannot pass the true cost of their production onto others and make other people poorer in that process. Somewhere along the line someone has to pay. The only problem is that everyone else is paying the price, whilst large multinational palm oil companies get rich. Interestingly, many of these companies are ultimately foreign owned so even Indonesia does not directly benefit. Ultimately all of the devastation of the rainforest comes at an extremely high price to the planet.

New Truism: Therefore, palm oil is definitely one of the most expensive products in the world today.

Furthermore, one of the main drivers for palm oil companies to clear and destroy existing rainforest, instead of simply re-planting already cleared land with palm trees, is that they sell the wood from the trees they clear, for a profit. Thereby funding their destruction and literally being paid to annihilate precious rainforest habitat. Once again, I state that palm oil is one of the most costly products on the market today, and this madness makes neither *sense nor cents* for anyone except an elite few.

Stop Buying Palm Oil Products to Fix the Problem...

Truism: We can save orangutans by not buying products containing palm oil. After hearing the previous example I understand that for many people it would be easy to jump to the conclusion that we can save the orangutans by just checking our purchases at the supermarket and choosing not to buy products containing palm oil. However, from experience, I know that this is not the case.

Question to Find Untruth: In fact, I get somewhat frustrated that I cannot dispel the overly simplistic view point of individuals who think the situation will change for orangutans if we just stop buying palm oil products. The reason being, that we must question how this works on a practical basis? Because, in reality, this view point is misguided in many ways.

Evidence of Falsity: Firstly, there is a driver for the forest to be destroyed just for the value of the timber. So to think that banning a later grown product will necessarily stop the greed, is incorrect. Therefore, your mother was wrong when she told you that, *money doesn't grow on trees,* because the opposite is true and *money literally does grow on trees!*

What is required, however, are proactive steps to protect and secure the forest before the companies get anywhere near it. The only way to do this is to use science, public scrutiny and representation to change land-use planning and raise funds to buy or lease the land. Followed by effective on-the-ground protection, linked to community benefit and engagement. Therefore donations to support these initiatives are the number one way to save the orangutans and the forests.

Furthermore, if palm oil was banned, the rainforest would most likely be replaced for some other profit-making resource or crop such as rubber, pulp paper, or even coconut. So, if you want to live an environmentally neutral life, the best thing you can do is to contribute directly to the orangutans or to saving the forest, their natural habitat. These are the types of steps which are going to make a real difference.

New Truism: You can save the orangutans and the rainforest by donating directly to secure, conserve and protect the natural habitat.

Interestingly, running a campaign against a particular company doesn't work either as there are many other companies ready to replace them. The only effective campaign against a company would be to drive change in their land management of existing concessions within a targeted ecosystem.

We Can't Afford to Save the Rainforest …

Truism: It will cost too much money to save the orangutans and it is money which we don't have as a society. Once some people hear about the challenges of the situation and the complexity of our work to save orangutans, they throw their hands up into the air and say, "*It's all too hard.*" Plus, they complain that it will simply cost too much money for us as a society, to achieve our aims.

Question to Find Untruth: However, is this actually true? Surely this depends upon that which you are already spending your money, and also on what you consider as expensive. The truth is that we can't afford *not to save* the orangutans and the rainforests which support them.

Evidence of Falsity: There is a paradox on Earth which dictates that we spend billions of dollars upon space travel to distant planets within our solar system. We do this in order to explore and research to find evidence of microscopic life or perhaps water on another planet. Yet here, back on Earth, we destroy our own beautiful home, which is also home to all of the other species on the planet. We never question this expense nor consider that for a few million dollars per year we could easily save the orangutans, an irreplaceable and intelligent life form and, just as importantly, their habitat which helps us all.

Doesn't it seem strange that we have the funds to explore the cosmos and perhaps find another planet to colonise, if and when technology makes this possible, whilst we are still destroying our own? To me, I think that until and unless we can look after our own home and the other beings who live here, we do not have the right nor deserve to colonise another planet. Otherwise we will simply take the same destructive mentality with us and repeat the same mistakes on another world. Perhaps beings from another planet would consider our species as *space vandals* if they encountered us and witnessed our behaviour?

On the other hand, we also spend billions of dollars on wars and weapons of destruction to kill each other, when this money could be spent on conserving the environment. Many of these wars have been proven to be based upon lies and deception, rather than any real defence needs. These funds could also be channelled towards infrastructure, public services, social systems, education and health services for all humanity. Therefore the money is available, it simply comes down to the will and the choice to spend it upon constructive projects, and more specifically, upon the causes which will guarantee the health and well-being of our planet as a whole. Instead of focussing upon the destructive ones which borrow from our future generations and put them into environmental debt making it impossible for them to live on Earth into the future. Do we have the right to do this? The answer is, "No."

New Truism: The truth is that we can't afford *not to save* the orangutans and the rainforest which supports them. Because we know that to save the rainforests is to help save the planet.

A Question of Value...

I was able to glimpse a very interesting and rather humorous example of the differing values we have amongst humans and orangutans too, when I was leading one of The Orangutan Project's Eco Tours a few years ago.

At the time we had taken a small group of eco tourists into the forest environment in Borneo. As part of the tour we arranged for the group to complete a trek through some of the rainforest wet lands. This meant that, for part of the day, we would have to walk across a narrow wooden boardwalk along the trail due to the boggy and muddy nature of the terrain. Importantly, this area also contained ex-captive orangutans who now lived there after being released back into the forest.

Within the group was a married couple who were taking this tour together. They were both supporters of The Orangutan Project and loved orangutans. Because they were so keen to see and experience the orangutans in their natural habitat, the wife had invested in an expensive digital camera for the trip, which cost her around $3,000. So the camera came everywhere with her and this trek was no exception.

We were out in the rainforest and had come to the wooden boardwalk section of the walk. It was a narrow path, so everyone had to fall into single file to avoid falling into the mud along the track. All was going well, until I saw a large wild male orangutan walking along the same stretch of track some way behind us, but he was following our path and may have caught up with us if we didn't keep moving.

Therefore I continued to move the group forward, but informed them that we had a large male orangutan on our tail and heading our way. Everyone was coping with this news quite well, until up in the distance I saw a large female orangutan, who I knew to be unpredictable, sitting on the boardwalk... and we were going to reach her relatively soon.

I quickly considered our options and chose to keep our group moving forward towards the female orangutan, as she was a safer bet than an encounter with the male. However I explained very clearly to everyone in the group that under no circumstances were they to stop to look at, touch, interact with or try to "pat" the female orangutan as we passed her on the track. Instead everyone was to keep their eyes forward and to move past her with as little fuss as possible.

As we approached the female orangutan, everyone followed the instructions. All was going smoothly, until it came to the married couple at the back of the group. Unfortunately being in such close proximity was just too much of a temptation for them and they both stopped next to the female orangutan on the track. For a second all was fine, and then in an instant the orangutan grabbed for the expensive camera strung around the neck of the wife, taking hold of it with both her hands. Now instead of allowing the strong and slightly unpredictable orangutan to take the camera from her, the woman grabbed the other end of the device and started having a tug of war with the orangutan in the middle of the track. This only made the orangutan even more determined and she continued to keep her grip on the camera and tried to wrestle it away from the woman. This made the woman work even harder to pull the camera away from the orangutan. So there was almost a Mexican standoff occurring before my eyes, with both females refusing to release their grip on the object.

Remembering that we had a large male orangutan approaching us from the other direction and knowing full well the strength and determination of the female orangutan, who obviously wanted the camera and was not going to give it up without a fight.... I called out to the woman to simply, "*Let go,*" urging her to allow the orangutan to have her camera. However, in answer to this the woman kept on saying that she'd paid $3,000 for it and she wasn't about to let it go. Meanwhile her husband was standing alongside her trying to convince her to let the orangutan have the camera. However, worse still, I could see the female orangutan was pulling her opponent's hand closer and closer towards her mouth so she could give the inevitable bite to secure her prize. And this could have meant the loss of a finger for the woman!

As I observed the event playing out in front of me I was becoming increasingly concerned for the safety of everyone in the group, not just for the one group member fighting with the orangutan. I was still calling to her to, "*Let go... let go,*" and was just about to intervene, when I heard the husband say to his wife, "*Don't worry, the camera's insured.*" Hearing these words, a cathartic expression came over the woman's face and in an instant she let go of the camera.

The orangutan got her prize and holding the camera tightly in one hand, she proceeded to run off to the edge of the forest and clamber up the closest tree. When she reached a suitable branch, she sat down and promptly tried to sample the expensive camera. Realising that it was inedible and possibly hurting her teeth on its hard surface in the process, she then dropped it from the tree onto the ground nearby.

My relieved tour member scrambled over to retrieve her precious camera and was quite chuffed that it not only still functioned, but now sported an authentic set of orangutan teeth marks on the casing. Subsequently this meant that the camera had a certain *jungle cred,* which she was not unhappy about.

From this point, I moved the group on past the female orangutan, keeping ahead of the approaching male to avoid any further close encounters with the wildlife. However, the thing which struck me in that moment was how we can all be tempted to put the monetary value of an object above our own interests and our own safety, even potentially our own survival. It was clear to see that the owner of the camera valued the money she'd invested in her possession, the orangutan valued the thought of something new to investigate and I was valuing the safety of the whole group of people within my care. I suppose in this case, it simply came down to a matter of values.

(It also taught me that if I wanted to communicate effectively, it was important to speak to the *values* of the audience, not necessarily to *my own values*.)

Indonesia is to Blame for the Destruction of Their Forests...

Truism: We can place the full responsibility for the destruction of the Sumatran and Kalimantan rainforests on the shoulders of the Indonesian people. Or Indonesia and Malaysia when talking about the Bornean orangutans' habitat. This is often the first knee jerk response from concerned individuals, when they hear about the massive destruction of the rainforests. Firstly they place the blame on the people as a whole, and then righteous indignation sets in as they express their anger and outrage that this is allowed to happen to *our* global rainforests.

Question to Find Untruth: However, even though the clearing, logging and decimation of the forests is happening within Indonesia's sovereign borders, is it true to say that they are the only ones responsible for driving this set of circumstances? Because, I believe that what is happening in Indonesia is yet another example of developing nations being exploited by wealthy industrialised countries.

Evidence of Falsity: By looking a little deeper into the issue of deforestation within Indonesia, it is clear to see that it is based on more than just poor management, poverty and overpopulation in this region.

To begin with, the root causes were created many years ago and are driven by the centuries old impact of colonialism. As typically found in developing countries, Indonesia had its own indigenous populations who successfully lived within and managed the resources of the rainforests for thousands of years before colonial powers such as the Dutch and British began spreading their tentacles of influence and domination. Once the new powers set up operations within Indonesia they began to exploit its untapped resources, whilst at the same time working to remove the land rights and access of the indigenous people to their forest homes. So the once sustainable, self-sufficient indigenous communities were taken off their lands and the colonial powers turned the forests into agricultural production or mining sites under their control.

This process still continues, however, it is now often under the guise of *development*. I have come to know that Indonesia was initially colonised by companies, such as the original Dutch East India Company, so it has been *business backed by governments* entering Indonesia, not the other way round. Although Indonesia has gained political independence, it was born into debt to these old masters. A debt which has allowed the flow of wealth out of the country to continue.

So what we see today is, the developed countries continuing to consume most of their resources with the majority of the wealth going to a few. The statistics bear out that around 20 to 25% of the world's population is now consuming approximately 80% of the resources, with 1% of the world's population controlling 90% of the world's wealth. [21]

New Truism: Developed nations and powerful multinational business interests contribute greatly to the destruction of the rainforest, the loss of natural habitat and the drive to extinction of the orangutans within Indonesia. Therefore it is a global responsibility to correct this situation.

Seeing the Truth...

From the examples above, it is interesting to see how, by using critical thinking and applying the Socratic Method of questioning to our assumptions, we can quickly realise that what we consider to be the obvious truth, is actually not so. In my case, I'd like to share a personal story with you and apply the Socratic Method as the events unfold so you can see the process applied to a more personal way of seeing the world.

A Different Camera, the Rainforest and Happiness...

Truism: Material possessions make us happier.

From the moment I purchased it, I loved my new camera. Not only did I feel very happy with this newly acquired techno gadget, but I knew that it was going to give me the ability to take some fantastic photos of my trips to the rainforests in Indonesia. To add to the anticipation, Wendy would be joining me on my next scheduled visit into the rainforest, so the camera would come in handy for some holiday photos too.

Question to Find Untruth: But, was it actually the possession of the camera which made me happy? Because, I was happy before I ever knew of the camera's existence...I was happy before I purchased it and I was to discover, I would soon experience a degree of unhappiness due to my attachment to it. So perhaps the truth is that material possessions don't make us happier after all?

Evidence of Falsity: Our trip to the Sumatran forest was also an opportunity to share, with Wendy, the experience of releasing a male orangutan back to the wild. Due to the planned location of this orangutan's release we would have to transport him to the site by jungle trail and then lastly by river. When we reached the river we put the orangutan, who was inside his transfer crate, onto a bamboo raft which the Indonesian technicians fashioned from the jungle for the journey upstream. Wendy boarded the raft with him so that she could look after our belongings, and my precious camera. Once she was settled, Peter Pratje, the Indonesian staff and I pulled the raft along by ropes from the banks of the river.

Wendy was seated on the raft with the male orangutan and my brand new camera in her hands so that she could capture some pictures as we travelled along the waterway. With Peter, myself and the team moving the raft forward via the ropes, all seemed to be going well. However, I would say that less than two minutes after giving Wendy my camera I heard her scream and looked around with just enough time to see it flying through the air, only to then fall straight into the fast flowing river.

In shock and surprise I looked over to Wendy and asked, "*What happened?*" Wendy coolly returned my gaze and said, "*A spider landed on me!*" That was the end of my camera and my happiness about owning it. Feeling momentarily disappointed at the unexpected loss, I reflected that nature has a way of teaching us about the importance of possessions. And I asked myself, "*Was I still happy and was the loss of the camera going to lessen my enjoyment of releasing another orangutan back to his natural habitat?*" My answer was, "*No, not at all.*"

New Truism: It is not possessions which make us happy, but our inner appreciation of the gift of life and each moment we experience it. The saying I live by is "*It may be difficult to find happiness within oneself, however it is impossible to find it without.*"

CHAPTER 12
LOVE AND A CHANGE OF HEART

"What the world needs now is love sweet love,
No not just for some, but for every-one."
Burt Bacharach

As a child of the 1960's, I think that the legendary, award winning song writer of the era, Burt Bacharach, said it well, when he wrote the song, "*What the World Needs Now*." Because not only is *Love* the key philosophical insight that I'll cover in this chapter, it is also the reason that the team at The Orangutan Project do this work. In fact, love always has been and always will be the raison d'etre for our organisation…and this encompasses love for the orangutans, love for all living beings and love for the planet as a whole.

To be clear, when I use the term *love,* I am not referring to the limited concepts of romantic, ego centric or any form of conditional, self-interested love. Instead, I am talking about Universal Love or what is known as *love without condition.* For me the defining difference of this kind of love is that from this perspective, we care about the welfare and happiness of other living beings without any expectation of what we may receive in return. So there are literally, no strings attached. Because Universal Love is truly altruistic, given freely of our own volition and for its own sake…Universal Love is its own reward.

As I have recounted in the many stories shared so far, I have no doubt that this is the love which I have been privileged to experience in my friendships with both captive and wild orangutans. However, as Universal Love has no limits, this love extends out to embrace all living beings and their rights to live free from the suffering and cruelty inflicted by humans. Furthermore, it is inclusive, offered without attachment or jealousy and benefits all those who come into its sphere. Universal Love is also truly intelligent as it works for the good of all, so it is necessarily, wise, considerate and makes the greatest sense in any situation. This is why I wish to apply the concept of Universal Love to the issues of *Changing the Way We Eat* and *Saving the Rainforest*, because both of these practices are based upon this *love*.

Changing the Way We Eat...

In Chapter 9, I suggested that one of *The Five Things You Can Do, Starting Today* was to change the way you eat by becoming a vegan, a vegetarian or at least by greatly reducing your meat and dairy intake. I also recommended that you educate yourself about the reasons why this is the best way to go. I put forward this suggestion, not only for your own health, but for the sake of extending loving compassion to all animals as well as to ensure the survival of the planet. Because the truth is that, livestock agriculture, dairy farming and the intensive meat production industry are the source of most of the animal suffering and death in the world and the number one biggest contributor to global warming on the planet.

Furthermore, the supporting data is truly staggering as well as alarming:

- With over 65 billion farm animals being slaughtered every year to satisfy the demand for meat, which equates to approximately 124,000 farm animals dying each minute of each day, 24 hours a day. This figure does not include the slaughter of wild animals such as fish, crustaceans, marine mammals and game animals, and when we include these, the figures could be more than doubled. [22]

- These industries contribute anywhere between 18 to 51% of all greenhouse gas emissions around the globe. It is interesting to note that the emissions from meat production industries are far more than the emissions from all of the world's transport systems combined, yet it is never tabled for discussion when solutions for climate change and global warming are addressed. Which, alone, is curious considering its impact. [23]

- Plus the fact that these industries require large scale land clearing, water usage and grain production as food supplies for the livestock, making them the most environmentally costly industries on the planet. In fact if we had to pay for the real environmental cost of production for 1kg of beef, it would make the price prohibitive and the industry could not exist as it does today. [24]

What is important to note is that these facts do not take into account the immeasurable suffering and pain inflicted upon animals as a direct result of our choice to eat meat. Nor does it consider how many meat eaters are actually animal lovers who believe in conservation yet who support and take part in this enormous, but relatively invisible industry. However, as always it comes down to each individual to make their own decisions in this area. But, if you were like me, I had no idea of what was happening to animals on my behalf. That was until I came face to face with animal suffering, their will to live even whilst dying, and was able to see the harsh reality of it for myself.

"The love for all living creatures is the most noble attribute of man."
Charles Darwin

My Journey to Veganism…

As you know, for as long as I can remember, I have been an animal lover. In fact, I never grew out of the inborn effects of biophilia, or a love of all life. However, this did not mean that I have always been a vegan. Quite the reverse was true because, even though I loved animals, I was also brought up to think that the regular consumption of meat and animal products *was just the way it was,* or *normal.* My belief that meat eating was natural for humans was instilled in me during my childhood as I came from a culture which not only condoned the practice, but actively encouraged it. Therefore I was what you would call a typical Australian male, which meant that I ate meat at least two to three times per day without ever considering that for each plate of food I ate, animals were suffering and dying.

Furthermore, as I joined the work force, I chose to earn my money by working as a kitchen hand in a fast food chicken outlet, of all places. Which meant that I was literally surrounded by the dead carcasses of chickens for every minute of every hour I worked. Interestingly, it did not occur to me to question why it was OK to eat the flesh of chickens, cows, lambs, pigs, sheep and fish for example, but it was a disgusting thought to even consider eating the flesh of a dog, cat, horse or rabbit. In addition to this, as an animal lover, there was no way that I would even think about killing any of these animals myself. The thought alone was sickening. However, I was somehow blind to the obvious contradictions in the situation where I happily consumed the flesh of certain animals on a daily basis, yet on the other hand, abhorred the thought of causing the suffering or death of any animal.

So I continued to eat what is known as the Standard Australian/American Diet (it's not called SAD, by mistake) without any qualms until I was in my late 20's. By this stage I was working with a large range of animals at the zoo and was loving my work immensely. However, the turning point for me came when I was part of a team which had to euthanize an injured giraffe during my time at Taronga Park Zoo-which I have shared with you in Chapter 3. It was this encounter, and others like it, which shifted my perspective on the rights of all animals to live and their over-riding desire to stay alive. I realised that I would never again have an animal die on my behalf, especially when there was no reason for them to do so. This was because when I stopped eating meat and animal based products, I realised that *eating meat was a choice not a necessity.*

The Choice to Eat Meat...

As soon as I became a vegetarian, and later a vegan, I received the inevitable questions and concerns from family and friends about the wisdom of my decision. Most people were worried for my health and wondered why on earth I would make the choice to *give up meat*? Their reasoning was that humans had to eat meat to remain strong, healthy and fit, especially as I was an active young man. However, not only did I not curl up and die once I removed meat from my diet, I also did not feel weak nor I become sick, as was predicted. In fact the opposite was true, as I began to feel more energetic and a great deal healthier than I had in a long time.

Firstly, as a zoologist I knew that humans did not possess either the teeth or digestive system of carnivores, so our bodies were actually not suited to the large scale consumption of meat. If anything we were perhaps physically designed to be minor omnivores, with only the occasional inclusion of meat, much like chimpanzees, our closest genetic relatives. In addition to this, our cousins the orangutans, eat a predominantly fruit and plant sourced diet, with only the small addition of animal based food, such as termites. Even then, animal protein is only eaten sporadically and makes up less than 5% of their total diet each year. Yet, I also knew that orangutans were up to 7 to 10 times stronger than humans of the same weight, so the argument of needing to eat meat for strength and well-being was a myth. Not to mention that I worked alongside some of the largest and strongest mammals in the world, such as elephants, rhinos, large hoofed animals such as buffalo, wilder beasts and zebras, all of whom ate a purely plant based diet.

"There are virtually no nutrients in animal-based foods that are not better provided by plants."
The China Study

In addition, I discovered that there were many plant based sources for protein, which were easy to find and simple to prepare. And to my great delight, I also found that both vegetarian and vegan dishes were delicious. So as my eating habits changed and I became increasingly happier, healthier and more energised, I came to understand there was no basis to the idea that meat was a necessity for humans. More importantly, I came across research and information which demonstrated that diets high in animal protein and meat products were actually bad for our health. The chronic diseases of modern western populations such as cancer, heart disease, obesity and stroke were a result of the Standard Australian/American Diets (SAD), which are all high in meat consumption. Therefore I realised that the choice to eat meat was not only unnecessary, but was unhealthy too.

"People who ate the most animal-based foods got the most chronic disease. People who ate the most plant-based foods were the healthiest."
The China Study

The Contradictions of Why We Eat Meat and How We Treat Animals...

Once I came to see that I had a choice, I started to ask myself, *"Why was it considered OK to eat a chicken but not a dog, a lamb but not a cat, a pig but not a hamster or a cow but not a horse?"* As an animal lover, I questioned why I had been blind to this strange phenomenon, because I knew that I could not personally take the life of any of these animals. Yet I happily chose to eat half of the animals from this list for around 28 years of my life, but the possibility of eating animals from the other half of the list, revolted me. With my background of growing up in Hong Kong, where I saw people eat a wide range of exotic animal products, I would never have dreamt of eating, I could appreciate that these distinctions had to be culturally based. So even the choice of animals we bred for live-stock was arbitrary and based upon a particular ideology. Therefore, it seemed that I had been trained to eat the flesh of specific animals and to avoid others, as per the norms of my culture, and not based upon my own preferences.

However, when I discussed this with some of my meat eating friends, they all told me that meat consumption was a natural part of human evolution. They also used the example of our ancestors, the cavemen, who were known to eat meat. However, cave men were also known to commit murder, rape, infanticide and wage war upon competing neighbours. I couldn't see how their behaviour could be used as a shining example of what we should do as highly evolved descendants...this reasoning just didn't make sense.

"A man can live and be healthy without killing animals for food therefore if he eats meat he participates in taking animal life merely for the sake of his appetite, and to act so is immoral."
Leo Tolstoy

I also find it interesting that one of the main points which those in the meat industry put forward in support of their actions is that the animals in their care are treated humanely. However, does the definition of humane treatment translate to being imprisoned in factory sized sheds, in cages stacked on top of each other? For animals to be unable to put their feet on the soil, to never feel or see the rays of the sun and even be denied the freedom to move? As this is what intensive chicken, turkey, veal and pig farming practices dictate. Then perhaps I do not understand the meaning of humane?

For animals such as cows, sheep, and deer who appear to wander freely in pastures, we have all seen the massive trucks moving them to either slaughter houses or shipping yards as part of the torturous live animal trade. Their ultimate deaths in the distant abattoirs are neither kind, painless or without suffering, just ask one of the unfortunate workers who have to do this kind of work to survive. They too are victims of this brutal and cruel system, much like the technicians at the primate centre, they suffer from these horrific environments.

In fact, I have often suggested that if we located all of the abattoirs and slaughter houses in the centres of our cities and gave the buildings glass walls so we could all bear witness to what occurs in these places, then perhaps things might change? Because good hearted people would not and could not stand for such practices to continue, once they were no longer hidden and out of sight.

Acting From Love to End the Suffering...

Ultimately, by far the over-riding reason for my choice to stop eating meat, was upon compassionate grounds and my love of all animals. Once I had seen the truth of the situation- that it was *by my choice* to eat meat *I condoned* the large scale slaughter and suffering of living beings- I could see no justification for this position. More importantly, I knew that what was happening was neither moral nor ethical, so I had a responsibility to act upon this knowledge. Which meant that my behaviour had to change as I was no longer ignorant of the facts. I could not support the system which counted upon my ignorance to operate.

Therefore my choice to be vegan primarily stemmed from a position of Universal Love for all living beings and if I loved them and did not want them to suffer, how could I support a system which relied upon this in order to exist?

Interestingly, I also noticed a transformative process which I call the *Vacuum Effect of Increasing Values*, occurring within me at this time. This means that when we increase our moral standing we move upwards to a higher, more loving way of thinking and seeing. Therefore I never actually had to *give up meat* and there was no personal sacrifice on my part. I had simply moved to a bigger, more loving perspective and to carry on in the old way was no longer an attractive or a viable choice for me. In fact it made no sense at all and the thought of it was now abhorrent to me. So when friends and family asked me, "*If I missed meat?*" I could honestly answer, "*No.*"

For example, when we leave the toys of our childhood behind as we out grow them, it is not a sacrifice to put them away and move on to more interesting and rewarding pursuits. It is just a process of moving from one way of seeing to another. So it was that after my deeper appreciation of the sanctity of life, the mistreatment of any living being became unthinkable. Vegetarianism, and then veganism became the only way forward.

Furthermore, I found I was in good company. With some of the greatest minds, wisest philosophers and forward thinkers over time choosing to practice either vegetarianism or veganism upon grounds of conscience and love.

They include, the following:

Ghandi, Leonardo Da Vinci, Charles Darwin, St Francis of Assisi,

Leo Tolstoy, Plato, Socrates, Aristotle, Lao-Tzu, Confucius, Buddha, Plutarch, Mary Shelley, Percy Blythe Shelley, Clara Belton, Franz Kafka, George Bernard Shaw, Albert Einstein, Benjamin Franklin, Abraham Lincoln, Louisa May Alcott, Upton Sinclair, Ralph Waldo Emerson, Henry David Thoreau, Thomas More, Rousseau, Susan B. Anthony, John Locke, William Blake, Franz Kafka, Alexander Pope, Sir Isaac Newton, John Milton, Vincent Van Gogh, Immanuel Kant, Coretta Scott King, Rosa Parks, John Harvey Kellogg, Sylvester Graham, John Denver, Jane Goodall, Maharishi Mahesh Yogi, Paul and Linda McCartney, John Lennon and Yoko Ono, George Harrison and Ringo Starr. [25]

"The time will come when men such as I will look upon the murder of animals as they now look upon the murder of men."
Leonardo Da Vinci

Saving the Rainforest...

I am often asked, *"Why are you so focussed upon saving the rainforest?"* My answer is a simple one, *"Saving the existing rainforest in Sumatra and Borneo from further destruction is the quickest solution to solve most of the issues in front of us."*

I also see it as an act of Universal Love, as it works for the good of all. This is because it not only helps the orangutans, it also helps the indigenous people, the surrounding local communities, Indonesia and Malaysia in general and all of us around the planet. Through the protection of the rainforest we also save these last remaining pockets of huge bio diversity, and conserve what is recognised as the *lungs of the world*. These green belts of dense vegetation work to provide fresh air and pristine habitat for all of us. Rainforests, especially peat swamp forest, the prime habitat of orangutans, also carry major amounts of stored energy in the form of sequestered carbon and assist in reducing global warming. The forests also maintain the soils of the region and defend against erosion and degradation, floods and droughts, as well as moderate the temperatures of the area. Therefore we get *the biggest bang for our buck* by focussing our funds and effort in this area....it just makes sense.

It's key to remember that when we operate at this level, from the global perspective, that it is not about seeing competing interests of wildlife versus people or environment versus people. In truth, we are all interconnected and we are one when it comes to looking after the planet on which we live. There is a higher interest at stake, which belongs to us all and humanity ultimately gains.

Therefore, looking at it from the micro to the macro view, The Orangutan Project's work to save the rainforest has the biggest impact and equates to saving the whole planet in the following ways:

1. Save the orangutans and their habitat – because orangutans are persons and if we allow them to become extinct it is a crime against persons.
2. Secure the future of indigenous peoples.
3. Secure the bio diversity in the area.
4. Assist local village communities via sustainable agricultural practices.
5. Save the local environment and protect environmental services, because destroying it makes no sense.
6. Provide a sustainable economy for the people of Indonesia and Malaysia, rather than eating into their future capacity, which is occurring now.
7. Lessen global warming by maintaining the rainforest and peat swamps and the carbon stores contained within the forests and natural environment.
8. Ultimately save the planet and end the madness of habitat destruction and the act of driving sentient beings to extinction.
9. Avert a world-wide environmental disaster.

Therefore saving the orangutan is about so much more than the protection of an intelligent and sentient species. Saving the orangutan means saving the rainforest. Saving the rainforest means protecting the lifeblood of our Earth and in doing so, we save our planet for all living beings into the future. Although it may not be the easiest of tasks, it is the one which promises the most mutually beneficial outcomes, if we are to avoid an environmental catastrophe in the not too distant future.

The Legend of Easter Island...

Perhaps the legend of the inhabitants of Easter Island is one which best demonstrates how our choice to continue the destruction of the environment could translate for us on a planetary scale.

I'm sure you have heard of this remote and distant island located in the Pacific Ocean, over 2,000 km away from its nearest inhabited neighbour, Pitcairn Island, and situated over 3,000 km off the coast of Chile, South America. Approximately 160 square km in size, it was originally purported to be covered with dense forests of trees. It also had a select range of birds and smaller wildlife but was uninhabited by humans for thousands of years. That was until a group of Polynesians, known as the Rapa Nui, made their way there by sea sometime between 800 and 1200 CE.

This relatively small number of seafarers settled on the island and began to farm the land. As the story goes, these new inhabitants began clearing the forests, practicing a form of slash and burn agriculture. As they prospered from what they so eagerly took from the environment, they began to multiply and expand their communities across the landscape. Thus leading to further and further levels of clearing of the once dense forests.

As their culture evolved the Easter Islanders began to carve and erect enormous stone head statues, called Moai. Ultimately the large and imposing carved rocks numbered over 850 and were dotted around the island. However, over time the islanders found themselves severely over populated and faced with less and less forest to plunder. Until finally, they had cut down the last tree on the island.

From this time, it is recounted that the islanders fell into decline and began to wage war upon each other in an attempt to survive on the now desolate landscape. As conditions deteriorated the bloodshed escalated and the once thriving people were reduced to cannibalism. By the time Captain James Cook visited the island in 1774, the inhabitants numbered only around 700 after the once proud population of many thousands. Worse still, they were eking out an existence and barely surviving on what meagre resources were at their disposal. [26]

As the renowned anthropologist, Jared Diamond, explains, Easter Island was one of the greatest examples of humanity's self-destructive behaviour, which he named as "ecocide." Due to their rampant and wholesale clearing of the forests and the island's native habitat, the islanders consigned themselves to certain ruin. He goes on to say that by over exploiting its environment, this culture doomed itself to decline and destruction and it did not realise its mistakes until it was too late. [27]

So the question is, have we learned from the legend of Easter Island or will our own incessant push for the destruction of our forests and native habitats, spell the end of our civilisation also? Or perhaps we will see what we are doing to our home before the last tree is cut down and the final animal made extinct and make the changes which we so clearly need? Because if we do not shift our focus to the wider perspective and broaden our sense of love to the universal level, our story could well be the same.

"Only when the last tree has been cut down, the last fish been caught and the last stream poisoned, will we realize we cannot eat money."
Cree Prophecy

THE WAY FORWARD…

"We can now destroy or we can cherish—the choice is ours."
Sir David Attenborough, Broadcaster & Naturalist

During the writing of this book, we received the difficult news that the Bornean Orangutan had officially joined the Sumatran Orangutan on the *Critically Endangered* list. It was not the news that we wanted to hear, but it did confirm our worst fears…that time is running out for our orangutan friends and their natural habitats. Most importantly, we could see that, now, more than ever, they needed our help. Without a doubt, we know there is still a long way to go and more work to do before we can ensure the survival of our orange cousins. However, this is a mission which we will not give up on, because we know that we have already made some significant leaps forward.

In fact, as I reflect back upon my journey to save the orangutans from extinction, I am aware of just how far we have come with The Orangutan Project. We have been able to secure and protect areas of their natural habitat, work with local communities and organisations to improve conditions on the ground, help to rescue, rehabilitate and release captive and injured orangutans back to the wild, instigate changes at both the political, business and legal levels for orangutans' rights, and inspire thousands of like-minded people across the world to join our cause to guarantee their ongoing survival.

Furthermore, to have been able to achieve this, we owe a great deal of thanks to all of our donors, supporters, sponsors and volunteers over the years. As we know that without them, we could not do this vital work, because we depend solely on their financial support, donations, dedication and time, to continue with our conservation projects and critical initiatives.

We also know that our projects benefit not just the orangutans, because elephants, tigers, sun bears and rhinos are also on the *Critically Endangered* list in these regions. That's why we've teamed up with five other premiere conservation charities—the International Elephant Project, Asian Rhino Project, Free the Bears, International Tiger Project and Silvery Gibbon Project—to form Wildlife Asia, and address the broader wildlife conservation issues in this area. More importantly, to face the pressing challenges as one unified force and solve the issues which we still see before us.

Ultimately, we know that we have the right plan in place to achieve the outcomes we all so passionately desire. We also have the expertise and experience to resolve the issues and create the solutions for lasting change. Now we need you, because together, we can make this happen.

A Possible Future...

When I look to the future for the orangutans, my cousins, my friends, I wonder what their world will look like in the years to come. As I imagine the way ahead, I can't help thinking of a classroom of children with their teacher, perhaps 50 to 100 years from now.... And two very different possibilities.

In one scenario, the teacher is showing some old digital vision to the children and describing the beings in the images as the species once known as the orangutans. Explaining that they were part of the Great Ape family and closely related to humans. However, they were unfortunately driven to extinction by humanity's ignorance, arrogance and lack of compassion for their fellow beings. The teacher goes on to explain about how beautiful, intelligent and majestic our orange cousins were and how sad it is that the children will never be able to see and experience the wonder of these beings living free in their natural habitat. The children can't quite understand how their forbears could ever have allowed this to happen…that they simply let the orangutans become another statistic on the long list of living beings which humanity had consigned to extinction.

However, I also see a second scenario… one in which the teacher is showing the children some holographic vision and describing the beings in these vibrant images as the species known as the orangutans. Explaining that they are part of the Great Ape family and closely related to humans, and that at one time they were threatened with extinction.

However, the teacher turns to the class and says, "*But fortunately, towards the end of the 20th century a small group of committed individuals decided to save the orangutans. All over the world they received support from other concerned people and together they were able to protect the last remaining orangutans and their habitat. Today the orangutans still live wild and free in Sumatra and Borneo and if you are very lucky, you could visit their rainforest home to see them for yourselves.*"

Which scenario we leave behind is up to us… which choice will you make?

NOTES

Introduction

1. *Merriam-Webster Dictionary.*
   www.Merriam-Webster.com/dictionary/vivisection

2. *Wikipedia The Free Encyclopedia* Chantek *https://en.wikipedia.org/wiki/ Chantek*

3. Ibid

Chapter 1

4. *Predict My Future: The Study of Us* |Documentary | SBS on Demand - The Dunedin Study
   www.sbs.com.au/ondemand/program/predict-my-future-the-science-of-us

5. *Dictionary.com www.dictionary.com/browse/biophilia*

6. Wilson, Edward O, *Biophilia: Revised Edition,* Harvard University Press, Cambridge Massachusetts, 2011

7. Yeoman, Barry, *Why the Passenger Pidgeon Went Extinct,* Audubon Magazine June 2014.
   http://www.audubon.org/magazine/may-june-2014/why-passenger-pigeon-went-extinct

Chapter 3

8. *Wikipedia The Free Encyclopedia* Great Apes
   https://en.wikipedia.org/wiki/Hominidae

Chapter 4

9. Cocks, Leif, *Orangutans and Their Battle For Survival,* University of Western Australia Press, Crawley, Western Australia, 2002

10. Martel, Yann, *Life of Pi*, Random House Canada, 2001

Chapter 5

11. *Wikipedia The Free Encyclopedia* Mirror Test *https://en.wikipedia.org/ wiki/Mirror_test*

12. Ibid

13. *Wikipedia The Free Encyclopedia* Theory of Mind
    https://en.wikipedia.org/wiki/Theory_of_mind

14. *Wikipedia The Free Encyclopedia* Chantek
    https://en.wikipedia.org/wiki/Chantek

Chapter 6

15. *Wikipedia The Free Encyclopedia* Declaration of Independence
    https://en.wikipedia.org/wiki/United_States_Declaration_of_Independence

16. *Wikipedia The Free Encyclopedia* Woman's Suffrage Australia
    https://en.wikipedia.org/wiki/Women%27s_suffrage_in_Australia

17. *Wikipedia The Free Encyclopedia* Sentience
    https://en.wikipedia.org/wiki/Sentience

Chapter 11

18. *Wikipedia The Free Encyclopedia* The Socratic Method https://
    en.wikipedia.org/wiki/Socratic_method

19. De Botton, Alain. *The Consolations of Philosophy,* Penguin Books.
    London 2002

20. Ibid

21. Rainforest Information Centre, *The Causes of Rainforest Destruction*
    http://www.rainforestinfo.org.au/background/causes.htm

Chapter 12

22. Joy, Melanie, *Carnism: The Psychology of Eating Meat,* Talk McDougall
    Advanced Study Weekend, February 2012
    https://www.youtube.com/watch?v=7vWbV9FPo_Q

23. Anderson, Kip and Keegan Kuhn directors, *Cowspiracy: The
    Sustainability Secret* Documentary, Los Angeles, 2014

24. Ibid

25. ProCon.org. *50 Famous Vegetarians*
    http://vegetarian.procon.org/view.resource.php?resourceID=004527

26. Krulwich, Robert, *What Happened on Easter Island- A New (Even
    Scarier) Scenario*
    *http://www.npr.org/sections/krulwich/2013/12/09/249728994/what-
    happened-on-easter-island-a-new-even-scarier-scenario*

27. Diamond, Jared. *Collapse: How Societies Choose to Fail or Succeed.*
    Viking Press 2006

FURTHER READING AND VIEWING

Anderson, Kip and Keegan Kuhn directors, *Cowspiracy: The Sustainability Secret Documentary*, Los Angeles, 2014

Bullo, Kylie. *Reaching For the Canopy,* UWA Publishing. Perth 2015

Campbell, T. Colin and Thomas M. Campbell, *The China Study,* BenBella Books, Texas, 2005

Cocks, Leif. *Orangutans and Their Battle for Survival,* UWA Publishing. Perth 2002

Diamond, Jared. *Collapse: How Societies Choose to Fail or Succeed.* Viking Press 2006

Esselstyn, Rip. *Forks Over Knives: Documentary* – 2011 and *Forks Over Knives Presents: The Engine 2 Kitchen Rescue, 2011*

Goodall, Jane. *Reason for Hope: A Spiritual Journey,* Soko Publications and Philip Berman. New York 1999

Joy, Melanie, *Carnism: The Psychology of Eating Meat,* Talk McDougall Advanced Study Weekend, February 2012 *https://www.youtube.com/watch?v=7vWbV9FPo_Q*

Joy, Melanie. *Why We Love Dogs, Eat Pigs and Wear Cows: An Introduction to Carnism.* Conari Press 2011

ABOUT THE AUTHOR...

For almost three decades Leif Cocks has worked tirelessly for orangutans to improve their welfare in captivity and ensure their ongoing survival in the wild. As a zoologist, author, speaker and founder of the international charity, The Orangutan Project, he is a world-renowned orangutan expert and outspoken campaigner on their behalf.

Leif's years in the field have earned him respect within the conservation field. He has been a key player in developing conservation plans for orangutans and influencing positive change for orangutan protection and survival. Leif is also President of the International Elephant Project, International Tiger Project and Wildlife Asia.

A small population biologist and curator by trade; Leif has several academic qualifications, including a Master of Science, studying orangutans. He lectures at universities, is a seasoned public speaker, supervises university students and has published several papers on orangutans in peer-reviewed journals. Leif is also the author of the book – *Orangutans and their Battle for Survival.*

In respect to his professional, animal, human and financial management skills, Leif has been: the longest standing Australasian Species Management Program Committee Member; a Quarantine-Approved Assessor; Zoo Husbandry Adviser; Zoo Accreditation Officer; an International Species Coordinator; and International Studbook Keeper.

JOIN US AND HELP SAVE THE ORANGUTANS...

Yes, you can help save our orange cousins from extinction and conserve their precious rainforest habitat for the future generations to come.

How?

By joining us at The Orangutan Project today. The Orangutan Project is an inspiring conservation organisation which works cooperatively and collaboratively with a range of other like-minded organisations, both in Indonesia and Malaysia. This strategy has meant that we are recognised worldwide as *the premier* orangutan conservation organisation.

From our humble beginnings in 1998, The Orangutan Project has been able to provide over $10 million dollars' worth of funding and financial support to reputable orangutan conservation projects in the field. Our targeted, innovative approach has enabled us to fund vital, on the ground projects including habitat protection, orangutan rescue teams, education programs, orangutan rehabilitation centres, release programs, wildlife protection units, community-based initiatives and legal actions to defend and secure orangutan rights.

You can visit The Orangutan Project's website at ***www.orangutan.org.au*** to discover the many ways you can help us in our quest to prevent the extinction of these remarkable beings. Because, protecting wild orangutan populations and their habitat is the only way the species can be saved...and your support can make the critical difference in achieving this mission.